Praise for Carrie's Journal

"*Carrie's Journal: A Journey Through Life and Loss* is not a story about cancer—it's a story about love that refused to fade. When Jerry Pierson discovered his late wife Carrie's college journal, he uncovered more than memories—he found the voice of a young woman whose words would guide him through grief and toward healing. Blending Carrie's reflections with his own, Jerry paints a vivid portrait of their shared life—of laughter and loss, strength and surrender, and the quiet moments that define what it means to love deeply.

Told with honesty, humor, and grace, *Carrie's Journal* explores the uncharted landscape of caregiving, the heartbreak of letting go, and the courage it takes to begin again. A deeply human tribute to devotion and resilience, this is a story for anyone who has ever loved, lost, and learned to keep going."

— JULIE RYAN MCGUE, author of *Twice a Daughter* and *Twice the Family*

"Pierson invites readers on a journey through life with his wife, Carrie—one that may seem ordinary at first, yet within those quiet, everyday moments, he reveals the depth of their true love and unwavering commitment. Together, they face life's final chapter with gentle grace—a moving reminder that love's strength endures through loss and ultimately conquers grief."

— KATHLEEN SOMERS, author of *Barely Visible: Mothering a Son Through His Misunderstood Autism*

"Pierson's account of caring for his ailing wife goes beyond a mere description of a grieving spouse. We are transported through time from the moment they met in high school to how their relationship transformed through the years. With vivid recounting of trips, raising their sons, and moving through life as a military family, we fall in love with the Piersons, which makes their struggles through his wife's cancer all the more emotional. As a clinical research professional, Pierson offers a unique view on how we understand illness, choose treatment, and cope with the aftermath. This is a book that will linger with the reader for a long time after they finish the last word."

— LAURA GADDIS, author of *Mosaic*

"As a grief specialist, and as someone who has walked through profound loss myself, I found *Carrie's Journal: A Journey Through Life and Loss* to be a powerful and heartfelt tribute. Jerry Pierson has crafted something rare, a love story that doesn't shy away from the hardest truths of illness and grief, yet shines with humor, warmth, and resilience.

Through Carrie's own words and Jerry's honest reflections, we get to know a woman whose strength and spirit remained undiminished even in the face of cancer. It's both deeply personal and universally relatable, offering comfort, connection, and validation for those who have loved and lost.

Carrie's Journal: A Journey Through Life and Loss isn't only a tribute to one remarkable life but also a source of solace for all who are navigating grief. This book will stay with you long after the last page, reminding you of what truly matters: love, courage, and the strength to carry on."

— GARY STURGIS, Grief Specialist and bestselling author of *SURVIVING GRIEF: 365 Days A Year*

"Jerry's story is one of resilience, love, and the human capacity to keep moving forward—even when life brings unimaginable loss. *Carrie's Journal: A Journey Through Life and Loss* is far more than a memoir of grief; it is a tribute to partnership, purpose, and the enduring strength that comes from honoring the life of someone deeply loved. Through his words, Jerry invites readers into an honest and vulnerable account of what it means to live fully—through the highs of love and family, and the lows of heartbreak and healing. His courage in sharing both the beauty and pain of his journey allows others to see that growth, gratitude, and meaning can be found even after the hardest seasons of life.

At Odin CrossFit, we've had the privilege of watching Jerry continue that journey. He came to us during a time of profound loss, and through consistency, connection, and community, he rediscovered his strength—physically, mentally, and emotionally. Jerry embodies what we believe at ODIN: that movement, humility, and human connection can restore hope. His story is a reminder that no matter where you are in life's timeline, it's never too late to rebuild, to find purpose, and to live fully again. *Carrie's Journal* is not just a story of one woman's life—it's a story for anyone who has ever loved deeply, lost deeply, and still chosen to keep going. Jerry's words will move you, inspire you, and remind you of the power of faith, love, and community."

— ALLISON & JASON JACHOWSKI, Owners,
Odin CrossFit, Frederick, Maryland

CARRIE'S JOURNAL

INDIGO RIVER
PUBLISHING

Carrie's Journal

A Journey Through Life and Loss

JERRY PIERSON

Carrie's Journal: A Journey Through Life and Loss

Library of Congress Control Number: 2025928197
ISBN: 978-1-969935-09-1 (paperback) 978-1-969935-10-7 (ebook)

This book is based on true events reflecting the author's memory of them. Some names and characteristics may have been changed, some events compressed, and some dialogue recreated.

Editors: Anne MacDonald, Dianna Graveman
Cover and Interior Design: Emma Elzinga

Printed in the United States of America

First Edition

3 West Garden Street, Ste. 718
Pensacola, FL 32502
www.indigoriverpublishing.com

Ordering Information:

Quantity sales: Special discounts are available on quantity purchases by corporations, associations, and others. For details, contact the publisher at the address above.

Orders by US trade bookstores and wholesalers: Please contact the publisher at the address above.

In memory of

Carrie Ann (Ague) Pierson,

and dedicated to Fern,

for the grandmother she never knew.

To Dan and Ben,

so they can know more of the full life of their mother,

AND

for teachers and counselors,

for cancer survivors and their caregivers.

Contents

JANUARY 4, 1977

I got this (journal) last night. I decided that I'll write what I feel, so I'll always have something to look back on to remember days past.

I'm eighteen years old now—halfway to nineteen, and yet I have no record of my past. Sure, I know that on this date such and such happened to me, but I don't know how I felt when I was honored or perhaps defeated—from now on, I will.

Introduction

It has been noted that life is like a painting—made up of hundreds of strokes—each representing events, that when viewed collectively, portray a complete life. And over time, the details on that canvas often fade.

Such was my predicament one month after Carrie's death until a discovery changed everything.

Sissy, Carrie's cousin, found a leather-bound book while helping me go through Carrie's belongings. I wanted to clean out as much as possible to overcome the inertia that prevents many widowers from even starting. Sissy, as well as my sister-in-law Karen, helped me get organized. We were busy that day as the life of a sixty-four--year-old woman who lived in the same colonial house from 1997–2023 could accumulate a great number of things. But it was that one item stowed away in a bin from Carrie's past that caused us to pause for a few moments before proceeding. Sissy skimmed through the first few pages, put the book down, and told me to open it when I had time to sit down with some time on my hands—and perhaps a stiff drink.

It was a few weeks before I finally opened and read through the contents, which recorded events through Carrie's college years and into the first few years of our marriage. I found myself moving from the numbness of death into the downward spiral of true grieving. Accepting death was relatively easy, as no one would want to see suffering continue. Learning to live without Carrie was an altogether different and challenging task. Reading the pages of that journal forced me to confront conflicting emotions: the grief of loss, but also appreciation for the life I had with Carrie.

Finding Carrie's journal inspired me to record her journey through life and cancer as a mostly positive message, as that is the mindset that any caregiver needs to maintain their sanity. Along the way, readers of this narrative will learn how we came to be and how we stayed together. They will read about the many experiences we shared, Carrie's journey through cancer, and the unfortunate circumstances resulting in her ultimate demise—a death that we both eventually knew was inevitable, but an outcome neither of us wanted to admit to each other—until the very end.

In the chapters ahead, excerpts from Carrie's journal are inserted to help frame the story. Carrie also collected poems in the back of her journal. I used some of the poems at transition points in the book. I did my best to confirm authorship and obtain permissions for use of the poems, but even in this age of the internet and artificial intelligence, perfect information remained elusive.

The later chapters describe my sojourn through Carrie's loss. It is not intended to be prescriptive or a guide for encountering loss. It is just my story, and if it provides insight to readers on a similar path, then I am glad to have shared my perspective.

Part One

Transitioning Through the Complications of Life

I am myself
A person, a being, an individual
And as that individual
I have my emotions, my feelings,
And my flaws.
I seek not praise nor pity,
Only respect and understanding.
Do not try to mold me to suit your needs
Or standards . . .
To do so would mean the loss of my identity.
And I would no longer be me.

— ATTRIBUTED TO MARK R. MIKAL[1]

Cancer is a multifaceted disease that cannot be put into one box. According to Siddhartha Mukherjee in his book, *The Emperor of All Maladies*, cancer starts with an error in the replication of cells—a process that normally occurs every twenty-four hours in the cells in our body. And in the trillions of cells in the body, errors in cell replication are not unlikely. Fortunately, the body has defense mechanisms to gobble up those wayward cells. And for some people, that defense mechanism misses a signal, and a cancer can begin to grow. There is usually no rationale as to who "those" people are who acquire cancer. Sure, some may have smoked for years, thereby overwhelming those defense mechanisms, but for most people, it comes down to rotten luck. Such was the case with Carrie.

1 Excerpt from Carrie's journal, attributed to Mark R. Mikal. Although this poem appears widely online, any original publication details are unknown.

CHAPTER 1

Life Changing Events

Because we will walk it only once then how important is it that we should walk it with some purpose that we can call our own.

– **Author Unknown**

APRIL 9, 1978

I can hardly believe that this year has gone so fast. There are so many things I would have done differently—I guess hindsight is better than foresight.

Time is an interesting phenomenon. It has a way of running simultaneously fast and slow. Our recollections of life events sometimes seem like days ago, and at other times, as if centuries have transpired between important moments in life.

It was the summer of 2006. We had been married for over twenty-five years, and we were almost certain that we would remain in Maryland. We had arrived in 1997 for my assignment at Fort Detrick, and my Army retirement was on the horizon. Our sons, Dan and Ben, were making their way through college, having flown from the nest just a few short years ago. We found ourselves on a road trip when it happened—that moment that seems like it was yesterday.

While visiting friends in Hamburg, New York, Carrie developed an unexpected and severe uterine bleeding episode to the extent that she did not leave the car to take part in a street fair. Our host, Erica, stayed with Carrie to provide some temporary help until we were able to return to their home. Carrie had irregular periods for years, probably decades, and therefore, we brushed off the episode as a difficult transition to menopause. Life went back to normal, or so we thought. I should have encouraged Carrie to follow up with her physician when we got back to Maryland.

Hindsight. Always 20/20.

That episode was quickly forgotten until an evening in late January of 2008. By this time, I had retired from the Army and currently worked at the National Institutes of Health (NIH) in Bethesda. A much more predictable and stable job to ride out our "empty nester" years. So, on a very typical evening for us of watching TV, it was alarming to hear Carrie announce, "I am going to the emergency room." It was all made more disarming by the fact that she didn't look distressed. I feel I should also mention that we were no strangers to the emergency room, having raised two athletic boys. So, I knew it was not a flippant decision that Carrie would make without feeling it was necessary.

"It's not that serious," Carrie had assured me at the time. "And the urgent care clinics are closed. But something isn't right, and I am awfully uncomfortable."

I wanted to drive her, but typical Carrie, never wanting to inconvenience anyone, simply stated, "Don't worry, I can drive."

Carrie didn't want me to spend the night with her at the emergency room and also have to spend the following day with a long commute. I did not want to leave her suffering alone, but I knew, stubbornly, she would resist, so I reluctantly agreed to stay home.

When she crawled in bed later that night, she briefly told me that the doctor ran a CT scan and found what they thought to be ovarian cysts. The doctor recommended she follow up with her gynecologist. "Nothing urgent," she had assured me, kissing me goodnight. Half-asleep, and following Carrie's nonchalant attitude, I didn't give it much thought and easily fell back asleep.

A few days later, and after a few phone calls with friends, Carrie had an appointment scheduled to see Dr. Rachel Mandel. It had been a stellar decision on Carrie's part, having learned she came highly recommended in the realm of gynecology, which would prove invaluable in our too near future. However, it was early spring before Dr. Mandel reviewed Carrie's case and ordered more tests and noted that yes, these could be cysts, but that they could also be something else.

Maybe even cancer. That was the first time we heard that word.

Still, the cause of alarm had yet to be pressed. Dr. Mandel explained that she could schedule a hysterectomy and remove the cysts. But, just to be safe, the procedure would need to be done by a surgical oncologist—someone with additional training in the removal of cancerous tissue for the purpose of staging. This doctor's expertise would allow them to not only just remove the cysts but also analyze the tissue during the surgery to accurately determine the extent of the cancer, if that was in fact what we were dealing with here.

It had taken us months to get a meeting to address the cysts, with our lives continuing as normal, but now everything was moving fast. We quickly scheduled a consultation with Dr. Fouad Abbas in Baltimore, and surgery was on the horizon. But Carrie had been adamant about going to Columbus for Danny's OSU graduation in early June. Therefore, life took another slight detour from cancer, if only for a little while.

During the intervening time, we did our best to live as if nothing was going on. We didn't talk about any "what ifs," but I know I was thinking about it. In retrospect, it is obvious that we were each in our own state of denial. And at times, the state of denial can be a comforting place to live.

I realize that perhaps we should have talked about those nebulous "what ifs." Perhaps we should have been more deliberate, but neither of us ever wanted to think the worst of any situation. We were generally, but not always, positive people who remained relatively optimistic about life events. We never shied away from change. In fact we had to learn how to embrace it. As Carrie prepared for her surgery, and I prepared for another life-changing event, I found myself nostalgic for how it all began.

We never really grow up, it seems
We keep in our hearts our fancies and dreams
And in a corner tucked away,
Is the child we all were . . .

–Edgar A. Guest

JANUARY 9, 1977

Looking back, McDonald is the only place I would have wanted to grow up. It was small enough to know everyone, yet had enough variety in types that I could become pretty well acquainted with human nature.

Carrie and I go back prior to those journal entries from January 1977, starting when we were in high school in 1974. Much of how we started has to do with the dynamics of Carrie's origins.

Carrie came into this world in 1958, a very much wanted child. Her parents, Owen and Margaret, were over the age of thirty at that time, old for that era, so Carrie grew up in an extremely protected life surrounded by many family members and close-knit friends. Carrie grew up in the village of McDonald, Ohio—a small steel town nestled in the Mahoning Valley midway between Youngstown and Warren.

Carrie's parents met after World War II, while Owen used his GI Bill to attend barber school, and Margaret was working as a bookkeeper. Owen would later take night classes in business and get a job with the state of Ohio in the tax department but maintained the barber business as a sort of side hustle. Owen's barber shop became the place in town where opinions about the Friday night game, be it football or basketball, were expressed with either satisfaction or dismay. And it was common that many of those in the shop were present not for a haircut, but to take part in the banter. In addition, Owen collected and dispensed favors, similar to a mafia don, but without the horse head in the bed. Owen knew where all the skeletons in town were buried but exercised considerable discretion in his use of that information.

However, Margaret was the likely source of Carrie's prodigious mathematical and reading abilities. Margaret went back to work part-time in the mid-1960s with the McDonald Board of Education as the assistant to the treasurer and later served as treasurer from 1979–1984.

By the time Carrie started seventh grade, she was already recognized as the top in her class for mathematical abilities. Her group of friends included several other girls, and in the small village, she could walk to any of her friends' homes within minutes. Carrie's house on Garfield was about as far from the high school as one could get, so Carrie learned to walk fast. An interesting feature of growing up in McDonald was that the kids routinely walked home for lunch and returned within 45 minutes to start the afternoon schedule. Carrie played trombone in the marching and concert band, was statistician for the cross country, basketball, and track teams, and took regular piano lessons throughout her school years. However, it was on the synchronized swim club, the Royal Swans, where Carrie grew from the ungainly first-year "cygnet" as a sophomore into a more graceful "swan" as a junior as her body went through a major adjustment to compensate for her height.

Into this life, I entered. The Pierson family not so much moved into the village but invaded at the start of the summer in 1967. My parents married in the summer of 1951 after graduating from high school, and my oldest sister, Cathy, was born just before that year ended. You can do the math. Jack followed in 1953, Mike in 1954, and Diane in 1955. Skip a year, and twins Jim and I arrived in 1957. A three-year break, and Tom arrived in 1960, followed by Sue in 1962, Joe in 1963, and Ed, the youngest, in 1965 when my mom was two months shy of her thirty-third birthday.

The seven boys and three girls of the Pierson family could be found wandering just about everywhere in McDonald. Maybe not the youngest, Ed, who was two years old at that point, but the other nine of us quickly immersed ourselves in the many activities the town had to offer. To maintain some degree of sanity, which would later fray, my mother established a hierarchical structure where older siblings helped look after the younger, and the weight of that responsibility was taken seriously. Our dad, while teaching during the day and coaching after school, worked midnight shifts on the railroad, and a few odd jobs to make ends meet. Though not formally stated, an expectation was set that we would go to college or learn a skilled trade, and that we would figure out how to pay our own way. We all achieved that goal, and beyond. Three physicians, one PhD, one JD, two accountants, two nurses, and one master electrician.

Work was something that we were accustomed to from the second grade, when we lived in Niles and helped older brothers Jack and Mike with their paper routes for the local afternoon newspaper. When moving to McDonald, Mike acquired the morning route for the Cleveland Plain Dealer. We were up every morning at five and soon out the door, loaded with our sack of papers—Mike on his bike, Jim and I on foot. As fifth graders at that time, with clothes thrown together from this and that, we probably appeared like street urchins from a Dickens novel, dragging our paper bags through the pre-dawn village. Fortunately, Mike gave up that route within a few years. Jim and I turned to work as substitute paperboys with afternoon deliveries and helped neighbors with yard care or shoveling snow. By the time we were sophomores, we followed the path of older siblings into the fast-food empire of the now extinct Red Barn.

I dated a few girls, from hanging out in the park with a girl in the eighth grade to taking a girl to several movies and the prom when I was a junior, and a few girls in between. None of these would come under the category of serious relationships, and neither would my relationship with Carrie during my senior year.

Even though Carrie and I had crossed paths on many occasions during those years, I cannot recall much more than a cursory head glance—a "Hey, what's up?" I was more tied in with several guy friends, and when it came to doing things, when not involved in after-school sports or working part-time at the Red Barn, hanging out with the guys took precedence.

I was caught by surprise when I found myself in the early fall of 1974, in trigonometry class, looking at Carrie in a new light. Carrie's coke bottle glasses had been traded for contact lenses, and she continued to blossom between sophomore and junior years as her height grew. Though she was a bit ungainly and lacking in coordination, she was well on her way to acquiring a graceful swan appearance. And it was not necessarily the combination of a maturing body and legendary brains that was appealing, but also a certain amount of wit and self-awareness that made her attractive. She was beginning to emerge as a person to be reckoned with.

As one of several students who transferred to the high school from the Catholic school in the eighth grade, I was automatically assigned to the "middle" math class and not offered algebra. High-achieving kids who had made their way up through the public school and survived high math in the seventh grade were automatically offered a seat in algebra. The formula was not perfect, but it did have its merits. The nuns at the Catholic school were not known for their math acumen. Therefore, trigonometry contained a mixture of juniors and seniors. I sat in the back of the class and Carrie in the front—until my glasses broke playing football, and I was moved to the seat in front of Carrie.

I enjoyed sitting in the back of the class and sticking my head up from time to time to demonstrate I understood the material. Carrie, from the front of the class, was recognized by all as the top dog. When I got moved, we became somewhat competitive. Although she generally did better than me, we always compared tests. I would get some questions right that she would miss—mostly due to careless mistakes. While it was not uncommon for Carrie to make errors with easy questions, she intuitively understood higher math functions. She would take great fun in making gentle and sometimes not-so-gentle digs at questions I would get wrong. I would push back with comments on her own shortcomings, though they were hard to find. Prior to this year, I had assumed that Carrie was quiet and reserved. Wrong. Her good-natured ribbing would sometimes take the form of sharp stilettos directed at my fragile male intellectual ego. The sparring would continue on a regular basis, much to the amusement of our teacher, Mrs. Beck, who had a front row seat to our quickly developing friendship.

It wasn't until after Homecoming, though, that I got the nerve to ask Carrie out. I was not too concerned about rejection from Carrie, but I was apprehensive about her father, Owen. I understood Owen was a larger-than-life character in McDonald, and it was not known exactly how protective he would be when it came to his only child. To gauge Owen's outlook, I showed up at the barber shop for a few weeks to listen in on the post-game analysis. Owen would later say that he knew from my camping out in his lair that I had ulterior motives. It turned out that Owen (and Margaret) would be supportive as they soon learned that the sixth Pierson child in that huge Catholic family had some prospects in life.

Though I had not yet heard back on my scholarship applications to either the Army or Navy ROTC programs, just knowing that I had ambitions in a medical career field provided a degree of acceptability to Owen and Margaret—and Carrie. However, as the Pierson family could not trace our lineage to the founding of the village in 1918, we were considered outsiders. We did have some standing in the community, in that my dad had been a teacher at McDonald from the fall of 1959 until the spring of 1968 and was head football coach for the 1965 to 1967 seasons.

Football was an important sport for all of my male siblings, as we wanted to follow in our dad's footsteps. Our dad had been a stellar lineman and linebacker at Ursuline High School in Youngstown, graduating in 1951 and playing at Youngstown State before an injury curtailed his playing days. Football was part of the fiber of almost every community in the Mahoning Valley at that time, and every town took great pride in their school's team and the blue-collar work ethic associated with the sport. None of my siblings were considered physically imposing, but we were all scrappers. My brother Jack played college ball at YSU as a defensive lineman at a whopping 185 pounds—he had to be tough and scrappy. Was I tough and scrappy? Scrappy, yes. But probably not so tough.

So, it was only natural that my first date with Carrie was to a football game at Howland High School, where my dad was now the coach and her cousin Paul was on the team. I borrowed a car from one of my brothers—was it Jack or Mike? Nonetheless, no car expense, no football ticket expense, and on the way home, we stopped at the Red Barn, where there was no dining expense thanks to an inside accomplice. I cannot recall too much of what we talked about. I think we discussed how her cousin Paul was adjusting to life after moving from McDonald to the much larger Howland High School and about the future plans of our mutual friends. We did not talk much about each other. We parted on good terms. I thought it was a successful first encounter and that we would go out again, but did not make any definitive plans. Carrie and I would continue to socialize in class, and I started walking with her on the way home during the lunch break.

The next move in the relationship was for Carrie as a Sadie Hawkins dance approached. Carrie did not make that move until she caught wind that I had rejected an offer from another girl because I was anticipating Carrie's invitation. I was not averse to going out with the girl who asked, a fellow senior. It was just that I thought, as Carrie and I were exchanging barbs nearly every day in class, that she would ask me. I was relieved when she eventually did. We had a genuinely good time despite never having done any square dancing. The "caller" made it easy for everyone to quickly understand the routine. It was a very different scene from the typical school dance, where the boys are on one side of the gym and the girls are in the center dancing in a group. The caller kept us moving from one "do-si-do" to the next. The event included a mock wedding ceremony for the participants. Mr. Snyder, our algebra teacher and pretend minister, had the good sense to call us something other than bride and groom, but he did encourage couples to engage in a kiss. While that first kiss would not rock the world for either of us, I do recall a certain amount of electricity. Strangely enough, in that pre-iPhone era, someone caught that moment in a grainy black and white photo and smuggled it off to the yearbook staff. Yikes! While not the end of the world, neither Carrie nor I were thrilled to see that moment captured, as we certainly did not yet have any thoughts of long-term prospects. Fifty years later, it is not necessarily a treasured photo, but a pleasant reminder of our beginning *(see picture section)*. Thanks to whoever it was that took that picture.

After that event, Carie and I would continue to go out on a more regular basis, usually to a movie or to get some fast food. I also visited Carrie at her house once or twice a week. Owen and Margaret were always welcoming, and we would sit in their finished basement watching television. Owen, as was his custom, would ask Margaret to bring us all a bowl of ice cream at some point between shows. Later in the '74–'75 school year, I would become a fixture for Friday night dinner with the Ague family. In some strange way, it was a bit like being on the set of "All in the Family," at least from the perspective of the interaction of Owen and Margaret. And while Owen resembled Archie Bunker, both physically and in mannerisms, Margaret was similar to Edith only in the way in which she waited on Owen hand and foot. Margaret's attentiveness to Owen was at odds with other things in her character, as she was intelligent and, though warm and engaging, could be all business when working at the Treasurer's office. Carrie's persona was far from that of Gloria, played by Sally Struthers. At that time in her life, I think Carrie may have been aspiring to be more like Mary Richards in the Mary Tyler Moore show.

During the winter, I interviewed for both Army and Navy ROTC scholarships. A good sign was a request from the Army that I report to a reserve medical unit to undergo a physical. I also took a trip to visit Ohio State. My dad drove me to the bus station, where I took a Greyhound for a nearly five-hour trip that usually took three if driving directly along the interstate highways. It was an interesting visit as one of my dad's former football players, who now played for the Buckeyes, took me out for my baptism on High Street at the long-since demolished Heidelberg South. I was still only seventeen. ID? Who needs an ID when you are with a member of the football team? While that experience was appreciated, what cemented my choice to attend OSU was the opportunity to pursue any of a number of different medical professions.

Late in the winter, I volunteered to help the swim club as the light man for their annual show, which gave me time to walk Carrie home from her practice sessions. Helping with the swim show was just another way to have routine interaction with Carrie, as by this time, our shared trigonometry class had ended. I was on to Calculus, and Carrie was on to something called Analysis. Carrie had put in an application to go to a six-week summer computer camp at Hiram College funded by the National Science Foundation. She helped the track team as a statistician, which Mr. Clute, our track coach and biology teacher, appreciated. She didn't need much, if any, instruction and was dependable. And as I ran track, we would continue to walk home together after events. Of course, I would take Carrie to the prom that year.

In late April, the Army scholarship had been awarded, and I knew that my future at OSU was secure—almost. My dad was never a helicopter parent with any of the ten kids. However, when the ROTC scholarship was awarded and he learned of the places where I could use that scholarship, he was eager to point out that Notre Dame was on the list. Too late. My mind had already been made up. The one thing I liked about OSU was the option for several different medical-related fields, as I was not quite sure that I could muster the grades to get into medical school. It would be my association with Carrie's Uncle Bill that would motivate me to pursue pharmacy school.

After graduating from high school in June 1975, I was hired by the village for the summer to help maintain the park facilities. It was a great job in that we started early and ended early. On a few occasions that summer, I borrowed a car from one of my brothers and drove to Hiram to visit Carrie, who was living in a dorm room while learning about Fortran and Markov chains—a true nerd camp. The National Science Foundation had the good sense to make a concerted effort to include females in the program, as the subject area was male-dominated at that time.

When Jim departed for the Army later that summer, we had a going-away party for him at a local bar in Girard. Even though Jim and I would not turn eighteen until August, there was an unwritten rule that you could always drink with your dad—so my dad hosted our friends at his local watering hole. The next morning, I was to drive to Pittsburgh to meet Carrie's maternal grandparents for the first time. When the Agues arrived to pick me up, I probably looked like I had been up all night. While I didn't have a hangover, my sleep-deprived body was less than what Carrie expected for this introductory visit. Her mood turned sour and stayed that way for the better part of the day. Owen was chuckling, though. As a WWII vet, he understood some of the traditions held by guys going off to the service. Owen's best efforts to lower the temperature by recalling stories from his time in the Navy did not work, but the passage of time through the day was the ultimate tonic, a remedy I found worked for Carrie more often than not.

I departed for Columbus on a Saturday in mid-September in a beat-up VW van driven by my brother Mike with Carrie and my younger brother Tom along for the ride. We arrived at Park Hall, a men's dormitory, and my few belongings were quickly unloaded. Mike, Tom, and Carrie were soon on their way back to McDonald without any special farewells. I didn't spend any time reflecting on Carrie's return home and our pending separation. It was time for me to settle in at OSU—a task I took seriously as I appreciated the opportunity to go away to school.

During my first year at OSU, Carrie routinely sent me cookies, and we wrote regular letters. I had great college roommates—Charlie and George. In the end room next door were Steve, Paul, and Dana. We became good friends and have maintained lifelong contact. I kept my nose to the grindstone that year and rarely went out on the town.

While I was at OSU, Carrie was busy in her senior year and sorting through college opportunities. She took a trip in the fall with Owen and Margaret to visit the in-state schools (with the exception of OSU) and fell in love with Miami University. Carrie had a thing for the consistent Georgian revival architecture of the buildings on campus, whereas the other state universities had a hodge-podge of old and new architectural styles. She was also impressed by the track record of Miami for training future teachers.

Carrie's senior year of high school and my freshman year at OSU passed quickly. Carrie graduated in June as the salutatorian of her class, and that summer, she worked with programs for the kids in the village park. With connections from my dad, I got a job at a steel fabrication shop in nearby Niles. The summer flew by, and Carrie was off to Miami in mid-August as the university operated on a semester schedule. OSU was a quarter-term school, so I started classes in mid-September.

Carrie's Coming of Age College Experience (1976–1978)

Finding Carrie's college journal weeks after her death helped me understand just how much she grew during those important formative college years. I knew that Carrie was miserable in her first semester at Miami. She was assigned to a freshman women's dormitory that was several blocks away from the main campus. The building had at one time been an independent women's college prior to Miami going co-ed. As such, the dormitory retained its founding name: Ox College. Carrie was doing great academically, but socially, she felt like a misfit. Perhaps growing up as an only child in a small town didn't prepare her for the diversity of life found at a mid-sized public university. We talked several times during that semester, and while it was obvious that she wasn't happy, she could never fully express what it was that she didn't like. She frequently spoke of transferring but never pursued it seriously. Carrie was homesick, and home was more than a five-hour drive away. It was only through her mother's firm intervention that Carrie convinced herself to at least stay until the end of the first semester.

At Christmas her freshman year, Carrie received a blank bound book as a gift from her parents and started writing before heading back to Miami. Carrie would write forty entries dated between January 3, 1977, and February 22, 1983. However, thirty-one of the entries are from Carrie's second semester at Miami in 1977. Another four entries were written in her sophomore year, with only one entry from her junior and senior years. Carrie contributed four more entries after we married until that last entry in early 1983. At the end of the journal was a section of poetry Carrie recorded that spoke to her at that time in her life. Most of the poems did not have an attribution, and I researched to find the authors' names where possible.

Carrie's journal serves as the centerpiece to describe our first few college years, a pivotal time in our relationship. The journal documents Carrie's coming-of-age story. To this day, I remain amazed that the book survived over ten moves and frequent purges as Carrie would often declutter the house when the urge arose.

From the journal, I would learn that when Carrie went back to Miami for the second semester, she continued to struggle socially and had conflicting emotions about the nature of our relationship. Although Carrie was uncertain of her commitment to remaining at Miami, she applied for a resident advisor position for her sophomore year. While waiting on that process to go through, Carrie wrote about a terrible experience at a fraternity party, about watching other girls in her dorm drinking and smoking, about time passing by all too fast, fretting about her weight, and in general, just feeling like she didn't fit in at Miami. However, all that changed in March of that semester when she was selected for RA. Carrie's good choice not to be a party girl paid off. Even though she was inwardly anxious about fitting in, on the exterior, she had learned that the veneer of a serious student would make up for whatever insecurity she felt socially.

In the entries of our uncertain future as a couple, the dichotomous writing can be catalogued under the heading of "Wait and

See." Similarly, I was thinking along those same lines 120 miles away in Columbus. Carrie and I saw each other when we could, but the situation was hardly conducive to building a relationship, which, in hindsight, was good, as we both had much to do in the next year. When Carrie departed for Miami for her second year, she had already considered the possibility of graduating in three years. Practical Carrie thought it a waste to slide through a fourth year of college with a light load and put additional financial burden on her parents, while at the same time recognizing that she could capitalize on her earning potential by graduating in three years.

The 1977–1978 academic year was a good time for both of us, but not together. Carrie had a great time at Miami University. And at OSU, even though I was struggling to keep my head above water academically, I was having a great time socially. During that year, both of us were trying to figure out our respective futures as a couple. Carrie was able to go on a double date with a friend at Miami. I took a girl, Sue, from my pharmacy class out to see a few movies and a few study dates. We frequently walked back from class together as our apartments were nearby each other, but nothing more physical than a kiss took place.

Letter writing continued to be the primary method of maintaining our relationship. I am thankful that we did not date during this current era of social media and instant communication—not that I did anything that I would regret Carrie seeing, but from the potential suffocation of too much constant contact. Even though we were in an unstated exploratory mode, we had not given up on each other, but the exploration was an important stage to go through. If I were to retrospectively characterize our relationship in that 1977–1978 school year, it would fall in the category of a movie like *Sliding Doors*, a series of chance encounters where things could have gone any number of different ways. Of course, at that time, I am not certain that I was as philosophical. I, like Carrie, was in the "wait and see how things work out" mode.

As such, I had a decision to make as the Spring ROTC ball at OSU approached. The ROTC ball was not a mandatory event for me during my first two years, so I never attended. But it was considered a "command performance" for junior and senior cadets. Carrie was not able to make it to Columbus that weekend, and she knew that I needed a date. Carrie was reluctantly okay with me taking someone else, but wanted to know a few specifics, not aware that I had gone out a few times with Sue. Realizing that this was a pivotal point with Sue, I opted for a safer alternative. I asked Anne, a friend in the classic sense. As Carrie knew that Anne was light years out of my league, she was okay with my choice. Regardless, it was great fun watching the heads turn as I danced with Anne at the event.

And down in Oxford, the introverted Carrie, a college freshman, grew socially from that ungainly cygnet into an elegant swan—a person who radiated confidence, which made her much more attractive. The only reason I think she wasn't hounded for dates at Miami during her sophomore year of 1977–1978 was that the Ox College dormitory was so far from the main part of campus that she was not a known entity, and she worked a lot. Being an RA meant more than listening to the girls' problems—she had to sit at the front "bell desk" on regular shifts along with the other RAs, and her academic major was primarily dominated by females. Carrie did go out with her friends from Ox College, and I am sure there were guys around, but Carrie was not the one-night stand kind of girl.

Carrie's emergence from a shy girl in the autumn of 1976 to somewhat of an outgoing social butterfly by the spring of 1978 helped her with her next position at the Ox College dormitory—the role of the Student Assistant (SA) for the upcoming academic year. Carrie would be the senior Resident Advisor for the Ox College dormitory.

While I was happy for Carrie's selection to SA, as we prepared for the summer of 1978, I knew our relationship was at a crossroads. This time in our lives was not unlike where we would find ourselves later in 2008. In 1978, we were pondering our future together as a couple, and in 2008, I had a new job at the NIH, with one kid graduated from college and another well along the way. It was another time of change. And we were making plans as if things would continue on forever. Little did we appreciate that the passage below, which Carrie wrote in 1977 about the likelihood of our relationship, would also apply to the likelihood of our future in 2008, as her years would soon be numbered.

FEBRUARY 14, 1977

Will what we have last forever? It's so hard to say. We keep making plans and talking about the future, but I'm never sure if we'll go through with it! I guess I'll just have to wait and see.

CHAPTER 2

The Good with the Bad

When Bad
Pray for
Courage
Hope
Strength to Bear
Grace to remember good

– CARRIE'S ADAPTATION OF COMMON THEMES OF PRAYER

The day after Danny's OSU graduation, we were en route to Sinai Hospital on the western fringe of Baltimore. The cysts of unknown origin on Carrie's ovaries could not be wished away. They required removal through a radical hysterectomy—a procedure that removes everything—ovaries, fallopian tubes, uterus, cervix, and surrounding tissue.

The surgery took longer than I anticipated. In a world where time sometimes flies by, this particular afternoon seemed interminable. Having that much time on my hands would have resulted in too much negative thinking had it not been for Carrie's cousin Sissy and husband Mike. They came to sit and distracted me from going down any metaphorical rabbit holes. After what seemed like a lifetime, Dr. Abbas finally came out to tell us how everything went in surgery.

"The good news is that I found solid tumors that were removed easily. Each ovary had a tumor about the size of a softball, and there was a substantial endometrial mass. I think we were able to remove everything, but there could always be residual cells remaining. The bad news is that, given there were three separate tumors, this is likely cancerous. But we're going to need to wait until the pathology report comes back for confirmation." So much to unpack from those few sentences. It was too much to process in those few moments before I was taken back to the recovery room. Yet, my gut was already giving me the answer I didn't want to acknowledge.

I can remember holding Carrie's smooth, familiar hand in the recovery room. Given that Carrie had been under anesthesia for several hours, the post-op recovery was slow as the medicine took a while to work its way out of her body, so it was difficult to have a meaningful discussion. Despite trying to have a cheerful disposition sitting by her side, I knew that she could see through my poorly disguised optimism.

Thankfully, I was able to spend the nights with Carrie at Sinai, as all the rooms were private. There was a mostly comfortable recliner chair to allow visitors to sleep next to the patient bed. The hospital staff were wonderful, although as this was a teaching hospital, many residents paraded through the room at various hours, making sleep difficult. I remember all the "what ifs" that played on repeat during that time. I think that is why the room was mostly silent during that time, neither of us willing to share our thoughts on what could be next. As I reflect on that episode, I remember finding a quote in Carrie's journal that she attributed to Shirley Temple: *The God I believe in does not send us the problem; He gives us the strength to cope with the problem.*

When it came time to remove the drainage tubes from the wound, Carrie put her foot down as one of the residents fumbled about. Carrie demanded that the surgical physician assistant (PA), a person with considerably more practical experience than the residents, come into the room to complete the procedure. She'd had enough of being someone's guinea pig, and I couldn't blame her for that.

Transitioning at home was akin to walking on eggs. Neither of us wanted to express what we were thinking of the unknown. To ensure Carrie's comfort and to be nearby to respond to her needs, I slept on the floor so that my moving in bed would not be a cause for any discomfort. I also learned to administer the blood thinner injections and did so with utmost gentleness. Fortunately, Margaret was with us and helped Carrie during the day when I returned to my commute to Bethesda.

We went back to see Dr. Abbas two weeks later for him to inspect the surgical site and to go over the pathology results. Dr. Abbas got to the point, but in a most gentle way.

"The pathology report confirmed that the tumors were cancerous. However, your lymph nodes were negative. It looks like the cancer was contained within the peritoneal cavity, so this is technically a Stage 3 cancer. I recommend you follow up with a medical oncologist, as there could be trace amounts of cancer cells in the peritoneum. And you may also want to discuss the case with a radiation oncologist."

Time was still moving after we got the news, but it was as if everything was on autopilot those first few days as the impact of Carrie's diagnoses sank in for both of us. I remember Carrie's first words to me: "I could die from this." To which I replied, "That's not going to happen."

In the days that followed, I focused my energy on research, gaining as much knowledge as possible to ensure my words to Carrie were not false. I continually assured Carrie that anything is possible with cancer and that all my research into medical literature was mostly encouraging. At most, I was just trying to keep Carrie positive. "You're an Ague!" I told her. "Your family lives into their eighties and nineties." As if that fact could stifle cancer alone.

Looking back, I'm not sure that my words helped. I responded analytically when Carrie likely needed something more emotionally supportive, like when she struggled to figure out how to tell her parents or our children. Just the idea would bring her to overwhelming tears. So, in my effort to support, I called in reinforcements by the name of Sissy, Carrie's cousin, who had a gift of communication, especially within the Ague clan.

Sissy, a saint, agreed to go ahead of us to Frederick and delivered the news to Carrie's parents. I know it sounds harsh that Carrie and I didn't deliver the news in person, but after all our years together, everything we'd been through, when Carrie said she just couldn't do it, I knew she really meant it.

According to Sissy, Owen was traumatized, but Margaret handled the news in stride and did her best to calm Owen. And to this day, I think the news of Carrie's cancer initiated a spiraling downward cascade in Owen that contributed to his death four years later. He never seemed the same after the news of Carrie's cancer in 2008. It was as if time accelerated for him after that. The boys, busy in their own life transitions at that time, took the news in stride, believing that their mom was Superwoman and would overcome the challenge.

The decision to proceed with chemotherapy was easy. Yes, the surgery removed the entirety of the mass, but we were not going to gamble on the risk that cells might have escaped to distant sites outside the peritoneal region of the body.

It was later in July before Carrie was healthy enough to go to her medical oncology consultation. Dr. Brian O'Connor, a highly experienced physician, explained the standard first-line therapy of carboplatin and docetaxel, with the normal six treatments. Cancer patients are quite familiar with these drug names, as are most people who know someone who has had cancer. If this is the first time you are encountering chemotherapy drugs, let me just say that they work fairly well, but their reputation for undesirable side effects is justly warranted.

As the academic year at Crestwood Middle School was to start soon, Carrie took the step to pre-emptively get a short haircut so that the loss of her hair would not be as dramatic. Fortunately, by 2008, the pre-medication for nausea was highly effective, and the high dose of steroids caused Carrie to become Superwoman for a day or two, but she went through the typical crash after the dose wore off. By far, the biggest challenge was after the second cycle, when her body was not quite as capable of recovering from the hematologic (blood) effects of the treatment. Carrie needed injections to help restore both her red and white cell counts for the remaining cycles of the regimen. At one point, she had to be administered intravenous antibiotics.

Carrie did lose all her hair, but it would later come back in a very stylish, almost white color and thicker than her original head of auburn hair, achieved by the regular color applications of her hair stylist.

After the chemotherapy was complete, Carrie visited a radiation oncologist in Frederick who was downright aggressive about the need for radiation. His manner was so off-putting that we sought a second opinion. The second radiation oncologist explained that it would be challenging to target a particular site, as the removal of the cancer and lack of positive lymph nodes would be like shooting a bullet at a dandelion that had already blown away, and that the chemotherapy would have treated any cells that escaped. We stayed with this version of things regarding radiation—and we were glad we did.

Regardless, Carrie came out of the chemotherapy phase without too much damage, at least in the short run. Long-term effects would make their presence known years later. Most notably in the immediate effects, the chemotherapy experience left Carrie with what is known as "friable" veins, making it increasingly difficult to find a vein for IV therapy. While those veins would remain compromised, Carrie's overall status improved over the next six years with the "fried" veins serving as an occasional reminder to both of us of what we thought was a victorious battle over cancer.

Looking back now, over fifteen years later, this 2008 experience with surgery and chemotherapy appears to have had a somewhat minor impact. However, at that time, it was a big freaking deal. And now, it makes me appreciate even more how we had decided to move forward with a life together thirty years earlier.

A Decision to be Made Together (May–June 1978)

As the departure of ROTC summer camp in 1978 approached, I found myself at a decision point. What was my next move to be? A gamble for sure, especially considering the uncertainty of both participants. Most of my ROTC colleagues were headed into the Army in the summer of 1979. That sobering fact made me realize that even with lingering hesitancy about my future with Carrie, I felt I needed to make my intentions known. Collectively, we were headed towards a "fish or cut bait" moment in our relationship. I knew I liked Carrie very much and could see a future with her, and I knew that she expressed interest in being with me as I traveled about. But bridging the potential canyon that would exist when we graduated and went our separate ways was something that would certainly cut into the likelihood of an enduring relationship.

As we had only a few days together from the time spring quarter ended before I flew out to ROTC camp, I proposed on the night before departure. We went to a restaurant, The Ground Round, which was a bit more upscale than a pizza parlor. I didn't put the ring in her dessert or get down on one knee. These types of romantic gestures were not common in the '70s. And the tradition of asking the father for the daughter's hand in marriage was also not in vogue. Instead, I waited until dinner was over and began my proposal.

"Carrie, I realize time is flying by way too fast," I said. "Before you know it, we could be living further apart. While we could make things work out, I need you to know that I want you with me when I leave for the Army after graduating."

I pulled the ring out of my pocket and showed it to her.

"You don't have to accept this, and even if you do, you still have time to reconsider, but I didn't want this summer to get started without letting you know how I feel about us."

Despite Carrie's immediate acceptance of the proposal, I knew she was apprehensive about how the next steps in our life would go. I was just thankful she was willing to take them with me at that time.

We immediately went home to wake up Margaret and Owen, who were similarly excited for us. Even though we just came in from dinner, Owen ordered a pizza so we could sit and talk about what we were thinking regarding a wedding—a topic I'd thought little about in the few moments we'd been engaged, still reeling over the fact that Carrie actually said yes. But it quickly became clear just how important it was for Owen and Margaret to at least get some idea of what we were thinking before I boarded the plane for Seattle and Carrie was off to Oxford on Sunday. We provided Owen and Margaret with some degree of relief when we told them that the wedding would not take place until after I graduated.

Moving Forward Towards Marriage (July 1978–June 1980)

Unlike the summer of 1977 when Carrie went home to McDonald and worked two jobs, she spent the summer of 1978 giving tours of the Miami campus as part of the summer orientation staff and taking classes to remain on track for graduation in three years. Despite our engagement, the next two years would be filled with us both living independently of each other most of the time. I can remember all the small moments we tried to take advantage of to see each other. After all, we were to be married at some point. It was during these two years, though, that I learned just how much I was ready to spend my life with Carrie.

The 1978–1979 school year was much more relaxed for Carrie and me, as we felt the need to deepen our relationship and became committed to moving forward with plans. Carrie, in her correspondence to her mom in the 1978–1979 school year, was already selecting everyday flatware and sending coupons to her mom to procure on her behalf. This was the picture of a person who had set a course and was not going to deviate from that direction. Fortunately, no torpedoes came our way that interfered with her planning. A few mild wakes, yes, but no major threats.

The ROTC summer camp changed my thinking about the Army. Prior to the 1978 summer camp, I was not active in extracurricular ROTC activities. I showed up for class and gladly accepted the scholarship money. But beyond that, I saw the Army as a four-year obligation. The summer at Fort Lewis changed my outlook, not dramatically, but I had fun and enjoyed the Army camaraderie. Consequently, I kept an open mind about my future in the Army.

At Miami, Carrie was busy with her role in the dormitory and jamming down the number of courses needed to graduate in three years. For the OSU ROTC ball at the beginning of February, Carrie was without transportation, so I drove down to Oxford on an early Friday afternoon in a borrowed car. Her friends acted like a pit crew at NASCAR and helped get her, the luggage, and a garment bag for the dress into the car in no time flat, so we could quickly return to Columbus to make it to the event that night. Carrie wore a "wow" pink gown lent to her by a friend, and in 1979, Carrie was the one turning heads at the ROTC ball. If the expression "outkicked the coverage" was in use in those days, the ROTC guys would certainly have been saying that about me.

Carrie came up to Columbus during my 1979 spring break as I stayed to work in the organic chemistry labs. I had a part-time job as the "reagent guy," and the school break was a good time to clean up the lab and make a few extra bucks. I made dinner for Carrie that night, a proud accomplishment. We had the entire townhouse to ourselves as the guys were away. After dinner, we watched special coverage of the Three-Mile Island Nuclear Power Station meltdown story. Decades later, we would be similarly intrigued by a dramatic mini-series of the Chernobyl disaster. At neither time would we appreciate the destructive power of radiation, even when used in a specifically directed dosage for cancer treatment.

Carrie graduated in early May (Magna Cum Laude). Regardless of her difficult start adjusting to the social life at Miami, the bulk of her time in Oxford had been tremendously rewarding.

Carrie's positive college experience, while only three years, and my great five years at Ohio State proved to be good for each of us in special ways.

Carrie and I took road trips to Chicago, Ironton, and Gallipolis for weddings in the summer of 1979. On the drive to Ironton, we spent the nearly five-hour drive talking nonstop about the future. Carrie initiated a roundabout process of getting me to consider my plans about the Army. She started slowly by opening with questions on the coming academic year:

Who would I catch rides from to go back to McDonald?

How often would I go back?

What did I think about my pharmacy board exam?

What would happen in the Army assignment process?

What kind of places would the Army send us?

How long would we stay at the first assignment?

Would we consider a second assignment?

It was a fun discussion talking about things for which we did not yet know all the answers.

We stopped in Ironton to retrieve my OSU friend Nick for the ride to Gallipolis, as we were to spend the night at the home of Nick's parents. After cleaning up in Ironton, we set out for the wedding with Carrie not completely ready. En route, she spilled makeup on her dress, and to Nick's credit, he recently recalled a most interesting statement Carrie made that day:

"Oops! Oh well, at least I'm not the bride tonight and no one will be looking at me."

Nick thought that was quite a display of self-awareness, as most young women at that point in their lives would have been mortified at the thought of showing up with an incompletely cleared stain on their dress. That was my Carrie. Maybe not all of the time, but most of the time.

Later that year, Owen and Margaret wanted to have my parents over for dinner so that they could discuss our wedding plans. My mom's mental health problems had begun to emerge, so she politely declined, but my dad wanted to attend. My brother Jack thought it was time to let Owen and Margaret know of potential problems with my mom. Jack knew Owen better than any of my siblings, as he regularly visited the barber shop and thought the best thing to do was to come clean with Owen and Margaret about my mom's personality. At that time, we didn't have a psychiatrist in the family who could pinpoint the diagnosis. That would happen twelve years later when my brother Ed finished his residency. But we knew something wasn't right, even though we always pretended that all was well at the Pierson home and that our mother was just shy. On a Saturday afternoon, Jack sat with Owen, Margaret, Carrie, and me to explain in concrete terms that my mom was not mentally stable, an accurate but non-medical assessment. Owen stated that he knew for years that something wasn't right with my mom. I felt a bit awkward that in the previous five years of our relationship, I had not been forthcoming about my mom, but I was relieved that Jack had opened the door so that Owen and Margaret could lower their expectations of the involvement of my parents in the wedding planning.

Owen and Margaret never let on to any of their friends that they knew of that skeleton in our family closet. Years later, my siblings and I would learn to talk more freely about mental health as we came to understand that keeping it hidden was part of the problem.

Carrie spent the 1979–1980 academic year teaching at Southside Junior High in Columbiana, Ohio, experiencing the normal ups and downs of a first-year teacher. These were growth opportunities for her. Most importantly, she ended the year feeling confident, which would help her as we moved to various Army assignments. Carrie would pass along a few interesting stories and experiences sitting around the Ague dinner table. One I vividly recall came from early in the year. A local church in Columbiana sponsored a family of Vietnamese boat people, and one of the kids ended up in Carrie's math class. According to Carrie, the principal arrived during the first class of the morning to introduce the child to Carrie and the classroom. There was little time left in the period to do much else, and as the next class for the new student was gym, Carrie asked a boy by the name of John to take the new student to gym class. Carrie, uncertain of the boy's English skills, felt the need to repeat herself several times to make sure the boy understood.

"John is going to take you to the gym," she repeated three times.

A moment later, a kid in the back of the class raised his hand and said, "My name is Jim, and I can take him to the John when he needs it."

Carrie practically wet her pants retelling that story.

In April that year, an event occurred that tested Carrie's emotional flexibility. I called to tell her that my reporting date for Officer Basic Course was going to be at an earlier cycle than the one requested, thereby throwing our plans for a July 26th wedding off-kilter. The invitations had already been printed, but not yet mailed. I was a bit reluctant to call Carrie to inform her of this news. She had spent a considerable amount of time planning for this event. This was not going to be an easy conversation.

"Carrie, I got my orders today with the report date to Officer Basic and you're not going to believe what happened."

Silence.

"What happened?"

"Well, you remember I said there was a remote possibility that I could get sent to an earlier course?"

Silence.

Frustrated breathing.

Sobbing.

Click.

Fifteen minutes later, Carrie called back as if nothing had happened.

"My dad talked to the Avalon Inn, and they were able to change the reception to the 5th of July. Turns out that date was wide open, as who in their right mind would get married on the weekend of the 4th? Right? Of course, we still need to talk to the minister to see if he is available, but I think this will work out."

Owen and Margaret came to the rescue with a date two days before I had to depart for San Antonio. The only additional cost was the printing of new invitations. Owen's speedy intervention allowed Carrie to quickly crawl off the ceiling, and everyone was relieved.

A Wedding (July 1980)

I took my pharmacy board exams somewhere around the 24th and 25th of June, and afterwards, was able to start mentally preparing for the wedding—something that Carrie had spent the entire year planning. My ability to contribute to the planning of major life events would follow a similar pattern throughout our marriage, for which Carrie would often say out of frustration, "You just show up!" Guilty as charged. Part of it goes to my upbringing, where our family rarely took trips and did not have big events. I had no experience from which to draw upon, whereas Carrie had a much more structured and fuller young life growing up with Owen and Margaret, where things were planned and events didn't happen by accident. Carrie did spend a good deal of time with her mom planning the wedding and wanted everything to be perfect.

As the wedding day approached, my mother's mental health issues emerged again as she announced to me, on the day prior to the wedding, that she did not intend to sit at the front of the church with the family because the wedding was not taking place with a Catholic priest. Of course, this was a ruse as my mother had not been to a Catholic church herself more than a handful of times in our entire lives up to that point, though she did make us attend every Sunday. Ed would, in the early ninties, point to a page in the *Diagnostic and Statistical Manual of Mental Illnesses* that described my mother to a T: paranoid schizophrenic disorder with a side of bipolar trait. The book may as well have had her picture next to the text. Unfortunately, the disease went unrecognized for far too long, and as a society, there are many barriers to both accepting that one is mentally ill and entering treatment. Looking back now, almost five decades later, my siblings and I still marvel at how our mother maintained her sanity for as long as she did.

But other than the fireworks caused by my mother on the 4th of July, it was a minor miracle that Carrie was unglued for only about an hour that night before the wedding and calmed down when we went to see my maternal grandfather, who agreed to help moderate my mom's erratic swings. My mother could transition quickly, almost like a Dr. Jekyll and Mr. Hyde type character, to a perfectly sane and loving mom. For example, weeks before the wedding, my mom arranged with the ROTC department at YSU for my twin brother Jim to fly back from Fort Lewis for the wedding weekend. This was quite an accomplishment and a reminder of the intelligent, caring person that she was most of the time—except for when she wasn't.

Notwithstanding the minor turmoil my mother caused at the wedding—and it went unnoticed by most people—the day was a big success. The details of the actual wedding day went "poof" in my brain long ago. The next week, Carrie took care of the logistics of our first move and departed by road for Texas with my brother, Tom.

Thus, we began our life together—away from family and friends in McDonald, away from our college friends (from Miami and OSU, respectively), and in a new environment.

It was the best thing that could have happened to us.

And the subsequent forty-three years were possible because Carrie was brave enough to follow her heart and step forward into the unknown. Little did she know, as reflected in a journal entry she wrote shortly after we were engaged, that her desires for travel and independence would be granted, but in ways she could never have imagined.

JULY 19, 1978

I'm engaged. I got the ring a month ago (June 9th). At first, I wasn't sure—and now I remain not sure, but I guess that's normal (I hope). I know I love Jerry and we'll be very happy together, but I still have reservations. There are so many things I want to do and try, travel, etc.! I guess we could also do all that together, but I won't be quite so independent. I guess that's what making a commitment is all about.

JANUARY 31, 1977

Together we should have a great life. At least the planning is kind of fun! I'm sure the time will fly! It always does!

CHAPTER 3

A New Way of Walking Through Life

If you want to be happy
Begin where you are
Don't wait for some rapture
That's future and far
Begin to be joyous, begin to be glad
And soon you'll forget
That you ever were sad!

– Edgar A. Guest

The post-chemotherapy era of Carrie's cancer journey took us into a new appreciation of what we had together. Carrie was in relatively good health as she would soon be declared in remission. Our sons were getting launched into the world, we had many good friends, we liked where we were at with our respective careers, and we had a good church family. Life was good, and we appreciated it.

Danny found a pathway forward to use his college degree in social studies by quickly obtaining a master's degree in teaching and getting placed at a middle school in the Frederick County Public Schools (FCPS). He would soon meet his future wife, and while we found having him in the basement for a few years after graduation somewhat tolerable, we were also thrilled to have him launched when he departed. Ben, after transferring from Carnegie Mellon to OSU, fell in with some great roommates, got serious about school and fitness, and surprised all of us when he said he wanted to use his chemical engineering degree as a springboard to medical school.

Carrie and I enjoyed life's simple pleasures of being together, sharing dinner, and joining our Clover Hill and Crestwood friends for social activities. Carrie was active in her volunteer work and took on more of an advocacy role for battered women and in cancer support groups. I traveled quite a bit with work and Carrie continued to take other trips, frequently with Sissy. Carrie was able to remain an active counselor into early 2015 and made a lasting impact on her students and fellow faculty members. Life was good.

I will always remember my trips with Carrie during this period. We were fortunate, due to Carrie's careful budget planning early in our marriage, to be able to do fun things together as our circumstances later allowed. The "road" trips alone with Carrie throughout our marriage, whether we flew, took a train, or drove a car, were always a special time. Carrie was a great planner of activities and almost always knew in advance where we would eat or what sights we would visit.

Upon completion of chemotherapy, Carrie remained relatively on target with her counseling responsibilities at Crestwood Middle School. Shortly into 2009, we escaped to St. Michael's on the Eastern Shore of Maryland during inauguration weekend and stayed at a quaint bed and breakfast within walking distance of a very nice French restaurant. The getaway also featured one of the more bizarre encounters we ever experienced at a bed and breakfast. During the normal breakfast small talk with other guests about where we each had traveled from to get to St. Michaels, one of the couples noted that they were driving down their street just as the police were arriving at their house. Carrie and I looked at each other. *Were these guys serious, or was this a put on?* The wife must have read our minds.

"Oh, we needed this trip," she said. "Our kids have been driving us crazy for months. Always getting into trouble. This visit from the police wasn't the first time. We turned off our cell phones as soon as we saw the cruiser pass us!"

How do you keep a straight face when someone tells a story like that?

Carrie's follow-up appointments with Dr. O'Connor continued to be routine, and for all practical purposes, she was in remission. During that time, we were able to visit Montreal, Bermuda, the Finger Lakes, the Adirondacks, and Lake Chateaugay near my brother Joe's family, as well as Hyde Park. It was a busy return to travel after being sidelined in 2008.

In the summer of 2010, we took the boys (twenty-five and twenty-three at that time) to Arizona to visit Sedona and the Grand Canyon, and up into Utah to see Bryce and Zion National Parks. We ended the trip in Vegas. An unexpected bonus occurred on the first day in Phoenix. We flew in early, and Carrie and I needed time to adjust to the time change, so we decided not to hit the road. Instead, we took in a baseball game between the Diamondbacks and the Cardinals. The game got a bit tedious after a few innings, and we wandered outside the stadium to a club called "Cooperstown" that Danny had looked up in advance as a place with both a baseball and an Alice Cooper theme. We went in and asked to sit outside on the patio. We were informed that it was closed for a private event, but that there were tables on a balcony overlooking the patio.

The private event was a birthday party for Alice's son, Dash. We found that we were overlooking a stage for a mini concert that Alice did for Dash, followed by Dash playing a few numbers with his band. During the numbers played by Dash, Alice came upstairs to the balcony and stood directly behind our table to watch his son perform. We were about 40 to 50 feet from the stage. Alice looked proud watching Dash perform—an unplanned bonus memory.

After Ben's OSU graduation in 2011, he learned that it would be unlikely that he would be advanced off the waiting list of any medical schools. Ben wanted to get a master's in biomedical sciences to improve his outlook for the next admission year. Carrie was not thrilled with the idea, as we had already supported him for six years as an undergraduate. I was able to negotiate a grand bargain between the two where Ben would repay the master's degree tuition and go to work in chemical engineering if he did not get into medical school the next year. He did—and Carrie developed amnesia about ever being opposed to his plans.

The summer of 2012 was busy with the wedding of Danny and Rebecca. In October, Carrie was able to take a few personal days from school to go along with me to South Africa. I took a few days of leave en route to a research meeting, and Carrie went along with two of my NIH colleagues to Kruger National Park and the Blyde River Canyon. What a spectacular time for all of us. We dropped Carrie off at the airport in Johannesburg at the conclusion of the tour, and I continued back to Pretoria for the meeting. Carrie was more than just a bit jet-lagged when she returned to Crestwood Middle later that week.

To celebrate five years of being cancer-free, we went to Santa Fe and Taos later in June of 2013. The food was fabulous. We had a great time seeing the Georgia O'Keeffe home and studio in Abiquiu, took a trip up to Los Alamos, and saw the Tsankawi Ruins on the return to Santa Fe. It was a carefree time as we really thought that

Carrie was in the clear for the future. Looking back, I am glad we deluded ourselves with optimism, as worrying about the unknown things to come would have ruined that time together.

These were the salad days of Carrie's cancer journey. We thought they would go on forever.

And looking back now on the early days of marriage, I realize we were learning to walk through life together. We would grow and endure, regardless of the obstacles encountered along the way.

Our Early Military Way of Life (July–September 1980)

After our wedding in early July of 1980, I departed the next day for Officer Basic Course in San Antonio. Carrie departed at the end of the week for a rendezvous in Houston as she traveled with my brother Tom, who had flown up for the wedding. It was a few hours' drive back to San Antonio, and while I tried to lower Carrie's expectations during the trip, my efforts failed. The entrance from the parking lot took us up the back steps into the kitchen, which, even when clean, appeared dingy. And then there was the matter of the rusty hot water tank in the corner. And perhaps there were a few cockroaches. This was not the beginning of marriage that Carrie envisioned. But she decided to make the best of things—after she quit crying.

Carrie would forever refer to the San Antonio apartment as "the pit." The "pit" that we lived in can be explained by a couple of circumstances. First, I flew down to San Antonio and was without transportation. The Army sent the Officer Basic students to a hotel downtown and shuttled us to and from Fort Sam Houston that first week. I didn't think that would work when Carrie arrived, and during a lunch break, I walked to the nearest apartment complex from the Academy of Health Sciences—the schoolhouse for various courses taught on Fort Sam Houston. The place was a pit. It was worse than any of my college apartments, but not as bad as some of the apartments where my college friends lived. Ergo, my rationale for accepting such hideous accommodations. We could live in anything for eight weeks, couldn't we?

Second, I did not understand the Army's pay for temporary duty assignments (TDY). I thought my pay was strictly that of a second lieutenant, not knowing that during TDY, you were paid per diem to cover the living expenses of being away from a permanent duty station.

Could I have done more research about how Army life works before departing for San Antonio? Likely. But this was the pre-Internet era. I was also disconnected from the ROTC staff during that fifth year at OSU, and I was busy studying for my pharmacy board exam.

There were redeeming factors to us living in that dump. We vowed to spend as much time away from the apartment as possible. We explored San Antonio, went on weekend trips, went to the movies, and attended concerts.

One of our first weekend escapes was to stay in San Antonio as tourists in a swanky hotel along the Riverwalk. Carrie poked fun at me as she roamed around the king-size bed, demonstrating how a good bed did not automatically sag towards the middle like the one back in the flea-bag apartment. After visiting one of the many outdoor bars along the Riverwalk for the obligatory margarita, we got dressed up and went up to the observation deck at the Tower of the Americas at Hemisfair Park, the site of the 1968 World's Fair. As the restaurant slowly rotated about the axis, we leisurely enjoyed our dinner and continued our speculative talk about what our future held. It remained a mystery as two weeks of active duty did not pull back the curtain on the ways of the Army.

Carrie took part in all the social activities with the smaller clique that formed over that very fast summer. Wanting to mirror the social graces of her mother, she invited the fellow pharmacy officers from my course over for dinner one night. She went to great efforts to find the ingredients and put together an eggplant parmesan in the decrepit kitchen. The evening was a success, but I wasn't sure I liked eggplant parmesan—strange, as my palate generally welcomed most any kind of food. A week later, she made the dish again for just the two of us.

"You know, I am not sure if eggplant parmesan is one of my favorite meals," I said.

Cold stare.

Sheepish look in return.

Carrie responded, "Why didn't you say something sooner?"

"I wasn't sure when we had this with Terry and Christine."

"From here forward, you need to speak up one hell of a lot sooner about these things!"

An unnecessary admonition, as from that point forward, I don't recall ever not liking anything Carrie cooked. She continued to explore recipes and test how things would turn out, and I was the grateful recipient of her culinary curiosities. And later in life, my palate learned to appreciate eggplant parmesan.

While in Officer Basic, I was called out of class one morning by the chief of the pharmacy curriculum, who had a worried look on his face. He said he had bad news. I thought someone in the family may have been sick, given the seriousness of his expression. Turns out that my assignment was getting changed from Fort Carson in Colorado Springs to Fort Leavenworth. While we were looking forward to living near the foot of Pikes Peak in Colorado, and the few household goods that we shipped were on the way to that location, I shrugged and said, "Great, Fort Leavenworth could be a fun assignment." When I went home for lunch that day and told Carrie, she was initially disappointed, but then her eyes lit up as she figured out that we would be close to her older cousin, Carol Ann Bayer, in Kansas City. Carrie and Carol Ann were separated by more than twenty years, so it was kind of like having a young aunt living nearby. Carrie threw out her tour books for Colorado and started planning on a future living along the Missouri River in northeast Kansas.

Fort Leavenworth (1980–1983)

We departed San Antonio past the midpoint of the month of September, long after Carrie would have had an opportunity to get a teaching job. We found ourselves in a very supportive community, not only with our neighbors, but especially with my boss, Bob, and his wife, Pat. Additionally, the entire group of colleagues at that small hospital was great. Moreover, before we had been at Leavenworth for our first week, we were making the 35-mile trek into Kansas City to have dinner with Bill and Carol Ann Bayer.

Bill was the director of the Kansas City Blood Center, and Carol was connected to many civic activities. Daughter Judy was a freshman at Colgate, and Barbara was a high school student. The Bayers took it as their duty to introduce us to the finer things that Kansas City had to offer. We regularly attended the Philharmonic, had the opportunity to go to concerts given by Yo-Yo Ma and Itzhak Perlman, attended traveling Broadway shows, went to parties in fine homes in the Ward Parkway district, and rubbed shoulders with the governor of Missouri and future US Senator Kit Bond. And every visit to the Bayer home for dinner included an eclectic gathering of visitors at the table.

Our time at Fort Leavenworth was personally and professionally fulfilling for both of us. But it didn't start so great for Carrie professionally, and there was one event on her side that quickly resolved. While I was having a great time getting accustomed to working in the hospital, Carrie was trying to get our home in order. I usually walked the three-fourths of a mile route with the golf course on one side of the street and the national cemetery on the other. Upon returning one warm, sunny early October afternoon, I found Carrie on the verge of tears, struggling to put curtains up in the living room. Did I say it was warm? It was closer to a hot day, and Carrie was frustrated as she wanted everything to be perfect. Moments later, neighbors were at the door asking us to go to the officer's club for the "beef and burgundy" night. What a welcome interruption, especially when these neighbors suggested Carrie take a quick look at their place before we head out. It was far from the Southern Living appearance Carrie strived to present. We walked up to the club, which was situated on a short path up the golf course. A few other neighbors joined us. A glass of burgundy and the opportunity to get to know our neighbors better helped Carrie forget all about her perceived troubles of the day. She lowered her expectations for perfection—at least for that project. I perceptively helped her finish the job the next afternoon.

I found the opportunity to work in the healthcare environment to be invigorating, and I could not learn enough. Similar professional fulfillment would initially evade Carrie. She was frustrated with arriving after the school year started and was not especially fond of substitute teaching. It got her thinking about her career choice and whether it was a good fit if I stayed in the Army and moved around. For a brief time, she explored the possibility of going into nursing as she had taken many of the basic science classes while an undergrad at Miami. That line of thinking was abandoned when a long-term substitute position became available in the Leavenworth City Schools.

While at Fort Leavenworth, we took part in various activities available at the community center. One of those would be a class in investing principles offered by a local university. The class was taught by an adjunct faculty member who was a broker with a large firm, where we would continue after as his clients. We stayed with this guy until his retirement in 2000, and did well by his recommendations.

On the financial side, Carrie demonstrated that she was her mother's daughter. The old saying that the Scottish can make a nickel cry was a trait Carrie had embedded from Margaret's heritage—not being cheap but buying good things at the best possible price. Carrie determined that we should live on one income and bank or invest the other. We did talk about it, but Carrie's logic made so much sense that there was nothing much for me to say. Thus evolved Pierson, Inc. All kidding aside, shared financial planning and investing contributed greatly to the stability of our marriage. We didn't set out with specific goals to have x dollars within y period. Rather, we wanted to be responsible with our money, so that when the time came to have a family, we could safely live on one income while the kids were little and still have money saved to buy a house if the situation allowed. That nest egg would only continue to grow, even when Carrie was at home doing the work of raising our children.

During the fall of 1980, our social interactions with fellow officers at the hospital helped further indoctrinate us into the ways of the Army. One of our friends would routinely throw fun parties at his bachelor officer quarters, and he encouraged us to host a New Year's Eve party. By the early eighties, expectations of officers in the Army had evolved from hard working and hard drinking to just plain hard working with moderate drinking. A DUI offense would be the kiss of death for any career, so the rule of thumb was to never consume more than one drink per hour, or less if you intended to drive. It was a somewhat liberal interpretation at that time, as current guidance is no more than two drinks per night if driving. At that New Year's Eve party on the last day of 1980, I was not going to be driving as the party was at our house. I had more than I should have and ended up sleeping on the couch. Carrie said nothing. She didn't kick me out of bed. She just looked at me with cold eyes after the last guest had left. The message was sent—and received.

In the next school year, Carrie landed a full-time job teaching at Patton Junior High School on Fort Leavenworth. Carrie worked for a great principal who quickly recognized that he had acquired a bright, energetic young teacher. He was nothing but supportive of Carrie, thereby reinforcing her confidence. As Fort Leavenworth had a disproportionate number of officers, most of the kids were from high-achieving families raised in homes with a certain amount of self-discipline.

During our second year at Leavenworth, we acquired our first pet, Kirby—the wonder cat. The term "acquired" does not adequately describe the circumstances, as Kirby was given to us by the mother of one of Carrie's students, who happened to live nearby. This dear lady thought the nice young couple without children needed this kitten as a "test pet" to get ready for having kids.

No kids yet? Why not?

Good question. We were still very young, but in the Army society of the early eighties, there was an institutional tendency to start families at an early age. This phenomenon could have been a function of limited employment opportunities for spouses. Regardless, we got caught up in that thinking, even though Carrie was fully employed at Patton Junior High. We thought that would happen in the summer of 1982 when she learned she was pregnant, but

Carrie miscarried before the summer was over. The first signs of a pending miscarriage were discovered while we were driving from Seattle back to Leavenworth after having visited a friend in Juneau, Alaska, in July.

That summer, we took our first big vacation, a drive out west and a flight from Seattle to Juneau. Upon return to Seattle, we drove back on a different route, heading diagonally towards Salt Lake City. Carrie noticed the spotting just outside Salt Lake City. We stopped at the health clinic at an Air Force installation where Carrie was advised to get back to Leavenworth in due haste. The next morning, I dropped Carrie off at the Salt Lake City airport for a flight back to KC, and I got in the car and drove east along I-80, stopping for a few hours to nap before arriving at Leavenworth, where Carrie was in the hospital. The OB-GYN was well known to me, and he explained the practical realities of the situation. After he did the D&C, Carrie went home to rest for a few days and started preparing for the next school year.

It is interesting that the miscarriage did not make it into her journal. After a month of the blues, she was ready to move on and try again. However, the anxiety associated with conception made intimacy a bit more challenging, and there was always the interminable wait at the end of every cycle to determine if she was pregnant (or not). And a history of irregular cycles made the wait more nerve-wracking. We really didn't spend a lot of time rehashing the miscarriage as we frequently were told, "You're young, you have plenty of time to have kids, lightning does strike more than once . . ." and at some point in the future, we knew that would happen.

And as we entered our last year at Fort Leavenworth, Carrie made her last entry into her journal. A very brief note:

FEBRUARY 22, 1983

Yes, I'm still alive and still teaching at Patton Junior High.

The note was followed by a few big question marks. What to make of the question marks? Who knows? One of the regrets of finding the journal after Carrie's death was not having the opportunity to talk to her about many of her entries. I am not sure if the question marks were about her future in the field of education, but I am certain they were not about our relationship, as the previous entries are mostly about how she was fitting in as a teacher. But even that is a bit confusing to me as from all outward appearances, Carrie was doing well as a teacher, both professionally and personally.

As year three at Leavenworth ended, we certainly thought about staying in Kansas. I could get out of the Army and work at the local VA hospital, and Carrie could continue teaching. The employment situation back in Northeast Ohio was looking bleak at that time. We had great connections in KC with Carol Ann and Bill and a network of civilian friends in Leavenworth. Carrie encouraged me to at least see what the Army was offering next, and as it turned out, an opportunity was open to serve at Fort Lewis where I had gone for ROTC summer camp. The catch was that the assignment was not in the hospital but serving as the pharmacist for an infantry division—a role that had been on the books but not filled until President Reagan decided in the eighties that we shouldn't have a hollow Army.

As we pondered the opportunity, Carrie put it to me that as I had one year remaining on my ROTC obligation, it would be a great way to see if I liked the real Army. Fort Leavenworth, as nice as it was, did not represent the real Army. Yes, this nudge was another of Carrie's subtle ways to fulfill her wanderlust goals.

We made many lifelong friends at Fort Leavenworth. But the most important thing we learned during that time was that we would stay together for life. Even though we had several years of dating and engagement, we really did not know each other all that well before we married. On the island of Fort Leavenworth, we learned to swim together and did not sink. Of course, we would hit rough patches in our marriage, times when we didn't like one another for one reason or another—but by the time that we left Leavenworth, we knew we were in love. We did not know just how much it would continue to grow.

Fort Lewis (1984–1986)

We took off from Kansas City on Tuesday, the 3rd of January 1984 and went as far as Grand Island, Nebraska before heading into Wyoming the next day. It was winter, and we encountered some interesting weather as we gained in elevation. Howling wind both hampered our progress and cut into our gas mileage. There was a moment of crisis driving between Cheyenne and Laramie where things looked bleak. Twenty miles after we passed Cheyenne, as we drove uphill, Carrie asked, "Did you see the gas gauge?"

"Oh yeah, it's going to be okay."

"When's the next exit?"

"I don't know, I think the next big city is Laramie, and it's less than 50 miles."

"How many miles exactly?"

"Not sure, but we can make it."

Heavy breathing.

"Do you know how cold it is outside?"

"No, but it looks pretty cold."

More heavy breathing.

And then, as if by divine intervention, a sign appeared for an exit where we found a one-pump station and post office combined. Not sure that kind of establishment exists anymore, but it was a welcome sight for us, and an answer to our silent prayer.

When we arrived at Fort Lewis a few days later, we would live for the next month in the "guest house" in the center of the military installation, waiting for "quarters" to become available. As it was early January, getting a position with the Department of Defense schools on Fort Lewis was unrealistic, but Carrie did find that there were part-time positions available in the Education Center, where soldiers who did not have a high school diploma went through remedial training to receive a GED. This was more of one-on-one tutoring than teaching in front of a classroom, and Carrie found the position to her liking as she had other plans for our time at Fort Lewis—like getting pregnant. As it had been a few years since the miscarriage, Carrie went about making an appointment at Madigan Army Medical Center on Fort Lewis, where Ben would do a residency in preventive medicine thirty-five years later.

Carrie had an "in" with the ob-gyn clinic, even in the short time we had been at Fort Lewis. In her volunteer work, she made connections at the Protestant Chapel with women who took part with their spouses in the Officer Christian Fellowship (OCF) group. While we were still living in the guest house, we were invited to a potluck dinner at the chapel, where one of that group was an ob-gyn who would later deliver our first child, Danny. The OCF at Fort Lewis would initiate several long-lasting friendships, and while we were at Fort Lewis, it would be a source of many social activities, as well as spiritual growth.

Over the 1984 Columbus Day weekend, we took a road trip that made more than just memories. Friends Joe and Luralee invited us to travel to Leavenworth, Washington, for an Oktoberfest in the touristy mountainside village with Germanic roots. It was a beautiful drive through Stevens Pass on Route 2 as the leaves were at peak color. We had a great time, and I am fairly certain that Danny was conceived on that trip. Even though I knew that Carrie and her good friend Luralee had been praying for Carrie to have a baby, it was my understanding that it takes a bit more than prayer to make it happen. Carrie suspected she might be pregnant sometime during mid-November, but given the track record with the miscarriage, she was hesitant to make any announcements, even to her cousin Linda, when we visited Eugene, Oregon, for Thanksgiving.

Later in the autumn of 1984, I was prodded by a mentor to seek more challenging positions. I ended up moving from the 9th Infantry Division to the 62nd Medical Group to become a company commander for the 47th Combat Support Hospital. It was a fun and challenging time for a twenty-six-year-old captain.

In 1985, I was also in the process of applying to a program where the Army would fund a master's degree. Selection to the Army-funded program was not so much a matter of academic merit, but of how well the individual was doing in the Army. And strangely enough, even though I never thought of myself as an Army careerist, according to the standards of the Army, I was doing a decent job. As the master's program would not start for at least another few years due to my three-year tour at Lewis, Carrie mused whether she could get her master's degree at the same time. Our unborn child would be two by the time the education assignment started. It was a great time to make such plans, as we were young (still in our mid-twenties) and adventurous. But as with the old Jewish saying: *Man plans, God laughs.*

As we entered the spring of 1985, we took a ferry to the Orcas Islands and stayed overnight at a bed and breakfast overlooking Puget Sound. The trip was a nice getaway during the final few months before the baby's arrival, and was notable for a strange vision Carrie had that night. She woke me at zero dark thirty (Army speak for "the middle of the night"), looking out the window into the Sound, saying, "Look, there are whales out there!"

Try as I could, I could not see any whales. How she could even make such a claim on a foggy night still baffles my brain. We will chalk that episode up to the hormonal effects of late pregnancy.

As we entered the month of the baby's due date, my boss at the 47th, Hank, took me for a ride to the Tacoma Mall for some personal mentoring.

"Jerry, you know that Carrie is going to give you something special in a few weeks that you cannot do by yourself."

"Yes, sir, I did reasonably well in both anatomy and physiology."

Hank chuckled.

"Well, have you thought about what you might do in return—any special gift?"

"No, sir, but now that you mention it, that sounds like a good idea! But I am terrible at gift giving, any ideas on that front?"

"Jerry, jewelry is never out of fashion. Do you have your credit card with you?"

Before long, we were on our way home with a string of pearls.

Life skills mentoring that was not forgotten. Thank you, Hank.

It turned into a very long day on the 29th of June when Carrie went into labor. After reporting to the hospital before 6 a.m., Carrie was told to go home and wait. We returned late in the morning, and the first signs of fetal distress were picked up on the monitor. By mid-afternoon, Dave, our ob-gyn friend, noted that something called a meconium stain was evident. Dave was concerned that the umbilical cord was wrapped around the child's neck, and before we could blink, Carrie was in the OR under anesthesia, and baby Danny was born healthy.

The next year, with Danny in our midst, flew by quickly. The autumn of 1986 was uneventful, except for one thing. As it had taken us several years for Danny to join our lives, we did not consider birth control. We figured that, naturally, it would be some time before Carrie conceived again.

Wrong.

Carrie discovered that she was pregnant. Any plans for Carrie to go to graduate school were put on the back burner. God was laughing at our previously made plans.

And as fall turned toward winter, it was time to move again. But before heading out to graduate school, I first needed to go to San Antonio for a six-month school called the Officer Advanced Course.

San Antonio (December 1986–June 1987)

We arrived in San Antonio in mid-December 1986 to allow time to find a place to live prior to the start of the Officer Advanced Course. Things fell into place relatively easily, and before Christmas arrived, we were invited to dinner with the family of my soon-to-be sister-in-law. My brother Jack met Hazel in Warren, Ohio, as General Motors had hired Hazel out of the University of Texas to work as an engineer. By happenstance, the wedding would take place during that short six-month window while we lived in Texas. Hazel's parents, knowing that Carrie was pregnant and due in May, welcomed us as if we were immediate family.

Jack and Hazel's wedding in the spring of 1986 was a rare event when we didn't need to travel. The Pierson clan, as well as Owen and Margaret, converged on San Antonio for this milestone. Margaret returned in May to be with us before Carrie's due date to take care of Danny while I went with Carrie to the hospital during the delivery. Carrie, as with our encounter with Danny, woke me well before dawn to tell me she was in labor. Upon arrival at the hospital, they sent us home, saying that Carrie was not far enough along. We returned a few hours later, and Carrie progressed through a long day of labor, finally delivering somewhere after 5 p.m.

The doctor who delivered Ben was a bit of a quack—actually, an honest-to-goodness quack. Years later, we would learn that he submitted a diploma from a Mexican medical school that did not exist. The capacity to do background checks for credentialing was not as robust as with current web-enabled mechanisms. This guy somehow completed the Army ob-gyn residency program, so he did have some practical experience. A head scratcher. The faux doctor was also a bit of an absent-minded professor type who would confuse Carrie with an active-duty female officer. At that time in military medicine, it was not uncommon for active-duty soldiers to have their bodies used in medical training by special forces medics. When it came time for the episiotomy, the doctor had the special forces medic perform the procedure. I was of the mindset that this was great training for this medic. Fortunately, there were no misadventures, and Carrie was soon in a postpartum room. As both of us had been without food the entire day, the first thing Carrie asked me to do was run out and get us some dinner. I found a Chinese restaurant, and Carrie devoured the meal.

"You know," she started, "I think this is the best food I've ever had." It was an expression she would frequently use when provided food in relation to a stressful situation.

"Another boy," she continued. "Perhaps next time it will be a girl."

Pause.

"Are you going to eat that last dumpling?"

While I didn't respond to any of Carrie's musings, I also never gave it much thought at that time, as the delivery, though quirky, was otherwise uneventful. And unlike the C-section Carrie experienced with Danny, the length of stay in the hospital was substantially shorter. Before long, we were bringing Ben home to meet Danny. During those first few weeks, Ben, while a bit fussy, had yet to demonstrate his true tendency as an infant.

The Advanced Course ended in early June, and I was scheduled to attend another six-week training course at Fort Leavenworth. Carrie would be left behind in San Antonio to have the household packed up, then she would go to Ohio to spend the summer with her parents, with a two-year-old and an infant. Fortunately, Margaret stayed with Carrie after I departed, and they were soon joined by Owen, who helped direct the movers along with Carrie while Margaret kept track of the kids. The group, consisting of Owen, Margaret, Carrie, Dan, and Ben, all traveled to Ohio by air and upgraded to business class, thanks to Owen's frequent trips with the State of Ohio.

When Carrie boarded the plane with a screaming Ben, she overheard the flight attendant in that section say to a colleague, "Thank God I work business class and don't have to put up with that kind of noise."

To which Carrie promptly handed the attendant her boarding pass and said, "It looks like today is your unlucky day!"

Carrie quickly settled in with the kids on Garfield Avenue in McDonald and soon engaged the services of family friends to help with entertaining Danny as Ben required all her attention. Ben cried in the morning, the afternoon, and the evening, and would cry himself to sleep. It was nerve-wracking for Carrie. And to make matters worse, Carrie had to go to Detroit to find us a place to live and needed to take Ben with her in the car as he was still nursing. Owen did the driving and arranged for the two of them to stay with Owen's sister, Mary Margaret, in the suburb of Allen Park. Unfortunately, while the rental market in San Antonio was robust, the pickings in southeast Michigan were slim. Carrie found a ranch house along a busy street that sufficed. She did not really have the time or patience to be picky, and given that our duration for the assignment would be less than two years, she determined the choice was adequate. And it was. By now, the excitement of moving with the Army had lost a bit of its luster—at least temporarily.

Detroit (August 1987–December 1988)

I returned from Leavenworth near the end of July 1987, and we promptly got ready for the move to Detroit. Thank God for the support of Owen and Margaret. We also had plenty of help getting settled from nearby extended family. But it was still not enough. Fortunately, most of my classes were in the afternoon and evenings, and Carrie went about the business of finding a teaching position for the sole purpose of getting out of the house and away from Ben, the crying baby. She found, if not the perfect job, a job that met her needs.

Carrie's half-day schedule was at a school situated inside an ice rink in suburban Detroit, where she taught high school math classes to aspiring Olympic figure skaters. The classes were small, the expectations were low, and the pay was inconsequential, as the entire point for Carrie was to get outside the house. And it worked.

In addition to the part-time job, we realized that to get a good night's sleep, we had to be physically distant from Ben. We set up a cradle in the finished basement where Ben could wail all he wanted, and it would not affect Carrie. My office was in the basement, and I think my presence helped Ben sleep more easily. His nighttime wailing slowly diminished, although we never did move him upstairs to sleep. Why tinker with a solution that was working? The stress of the baby also put a major dent in Carrie's outlook on future children. However, we grew to mutually appreciate each other's dedication to work in complementary ways to overcome the challenges of our growing family.

Fortunately, we were also able to latch onto a good church nearby and quickly had a reliable social circle of friends. One of the families had a teenage daughter who would babysit. Getting out on a somewhat irregular schedule was an important aid to sanity. Looking back on that time, I wonder if part of Carrie's depression was related to life circumstances. While I initially thought it might have been postpartum depression, the situation was multifactorial: Carrie's stress of moving and finding a new home without me; the arrival of Ben who had a very different disposition from Danny; the temporary abandonment of professional goals, especially knowing she was far more academically capable than me; and the adjustment to a new community different from the military communities. The list goes on. Carrie never expressed that life was unfair, but that thought must have been going through her mind at that time.

One of the things I found after Carrie died, while I was moving from Clover Hill to downtown, was the greeting card I gave her at graduation from Miami. Carrie saved a few items that she considered keepsakes, and I was mildly surprised to find this card included. On the inside, I wrote that I would support her in whatever academic goals she wanted to pursue. I knew back in '79 that she mulled over the prospects of going to the doctoral level. Carrie could have accomplished that, but at some point in life, she determined it was not as important as other things. Carrie later found professional fulfillment as a counselor. We never revisited that time in our lives to rehash and analyze, as what was the point? We survived and moved forward.

Time flew by in Detroit. We stayed busy with school and the kids. In early December 1988, I took Carrie to the airport to fly to Baltimore–Washington International for house hunting in Maryland with her cousin, Sissy, which led to the start of their enduring friendship. Prior to that time, they had known each other more through Christmas cards than through personal experience. Sissy was eight years older, but now with Carrie at thirty and Sissy only thirty-eight, that age gap was not as significant and would become less so with each passing year. The similarities in family characteristics, both being mothers of two boys with similar outlooks on life, made them even more compatible. The Ague genes ran deep in this pair of cousins often to the chagrin of Sissy's husband, Mike, and me. Regardless, it was great for Carrie to spend a few days getting the lay of the land with Sissy.

The move to Maryland was staggered as we had both Christmas and a family wedding in Ohio shoehorned in between. Tom's wedding was a lot of fun, at least for three-year-old Danny, who woke up the next morning, came to breakfast, and said, "That was a great party. When's the next one?"

Maryland (1989–1990)

We moved to Maryland for my assignment at Walter Reed Army Medical Center just inside the northern city limits of Washington, DC, about 30 miles from Columbia. We soon considered ourselves lucky to find a rental house in a decent neighborhood that was close to Walter Reed.

The assignment to Walter Reed was for an additional twelve-month post-master's training program, often referred to as a management residency program. The assignment officer indicated that I would likely remain in the DC area afterwards, either at Walter Reed or one of the nearby installations such as Fort Meade or Fort Belvoir. Carrie, now feeling somewhat more comfortable with boys who would soon be four and two, started looking at options for graduate school. She was accepted at the University of Maryland for a master's in educational measurement, statistics, and evaluation. Carrie's analytical capacity would have been well-suited, not only for the curriculum, but for a future in that field. However, before the year was out, signs pointed to an assignment in Germany, and the question now was, would it be in Berlin or Würzburg? The pending move to Germany was great for Carrie's outlook on life, and her natural tendency toward wanderlust made her forget about graduate school. She quickly moved towards an evaluation of the relative merits of the two locations in Germany—Berlin or Würzburg. The Berlin Wall had just fallen, and while it seemed like an interesting place to live, Carrie advocated for the greater travel opportunities from Würzburg, located in northern Bavaria. And as luck would have it, that is where the Army would send us.

Before long, we were out of the house in Columbia. Carrie and the kids were safely ensconced in Ohio while I took off for Germany near the end of July. They would join later, towards the end of August. The kids continued to have fun in Ohio, doing things with Grandma and Grandpa as they were turning into their own little people. Carrie, now comfortable in her role as the mother of two rambunctious boys, had fun right along with them. This was a very different Carrie who had been miserable spending the summer in Ohio in 1987 with a wailing infant. This version of Carrie had learned to move forward in a new way and eagerly awaited the coming adventures.

The last three lines from the poem at the beginning of this chapter now come into focus:

Begin to be joyous, begin to be glad
And soon you'll forget
That you ever were sad!

– Edward A. Guest

CHAPTER 4

Accepting the Unexpected

It's a long road you walk if you walk it alone
a rocky path by yourself where the sun has never shone
it's a jungle if you walk in a hot, steaming crowd
it's a battlefield you walk if you're worried and bowed
it's a walk in a meadow
a day that should never end when we walk in the sunshine with our friends.

– Edgar A. Guest

Carrie's life journey took an unexpected turn late in 2013. We had thought she was no longer on the cancer highway at that time. We made a short getaway to Hilton Head Island after Christmas that year with Carrie's mom, Margaret, and our younger son, Ben. Our first two days were carefree and easy living. We walked the beach, explored the many shops on the island, and enjoyed the slow-paced island life. It all changed on the third morning when Carrie woke with severe nausea, throwing up, and complaining of a pain in her back. I didn't know what to think, and Ben was only in his first year of medical school, so he was not much help.

I took her to the local ER since the pain she described was similar to what I had heard from people who had kidney stones. After waiting for what seemed like the entire day, the doctor came out and said that the CT scan showed that she had either a tumor or a benign hematoma growing on the left side of her body. Hematoma, in layman's terms, would be similar to a blood clot outside the blood vessels, where a pile of gunk attaches and grows.

Carrie was beyond devastated. I was at a loss for words. What could I say? It would have been disingenuous to tell her that everything would be okay. There was not much I could do to help other than sit at her side and hold her hand.

We made our way back to the condo by 11 p.m. After a lousy night of sleep for all of us, Carrie felt good enough in the morning for our scheduled flight back to Baltimore. It was a somber return to the reality of living with cancer.

We followed up with Dr. Abbas, the surgeon, in early January. A scan determined that a surgical option was not possible due to the location of the tumor in relation to the psoas muscle and nerves. The psoas is a long, ribbon-shaped muscle that connects the spine to the lower part of the body.

Dr. O'Connor, the oncologist, ordered further diagnostic testing. More importantly, he spent a good deal of time explaining to Carrie that the return of cancer was not the end of the world—that she needed to develop a mindset in which she was dealing with a chronic illness and not a deadly disease—words that helped "center" her for the next six years. A biopsy was scheduled along with genetic testing of the tumor. At that time, no gene-specific therapies were found, and the recommendation was to go back on the initial therapy (carboplatin and paclitaxel). Carrie knew what to expect with this drug combination. Prior to starting the treatment, Dr. O'Connor, knowing the status of Carrie's friable veins, referred her to a surgeon for the implantation of an indwelling device called a power port that would feed directly into the subclavian vein, thereby avoiding further damage to the rest of her veins.

Throughout this chaos, Carrie and I determined to bring as much order as possible back into our lives. We took a short trip to New York right after the school year ended and before the chemo started. We stayed near the intersection of Lexington and East 48th. It was a bit of a walk to the Broadway theaters. Didn't matter. Carrie somehow had abundant energy that weekend. We wandered about town for a few days prior to seeing Bryan Cranston play LBJ in "All the Way." What a memorable weekend. It was as if the troubles of the previous six months did not exist.

Unfortunately, by late summer and after two chemo cycles, a CT scan found that the treatment was not having any effect and that the tumor was growing. Dr. O'Connor noted that radiation was possible now since this was a localized tumor, but also recommended that Carrie explore clinical trial options. This would be an avenue to gain access to immunotherapy regimens, as those were not yet approved for her specific cancer. Even with only two cycles of chemotherapy, Carrie had again lost her hair, and this time it came back even whiter but a bit thinner. And as with the first time her hair came back, Carrie could still turn heads with her well-maintained white bob and 10,000-watt smile.

Carrie started radiation treatments in the early fall and endured the new insult to her body. The long-term effects of the radiation would reveal themselves years later. Shortly after the radiation treatment started, I found through ClinicalTrials.gov a research study at the National Cancer Institute (NCI) for which Carrie met the entry criteria. For research studies, not everyone qualifies medically for enrollment. Think of the inclusion criteria as things you must have. For example, you must be within a certain age range and have a certain type of cancer. And for exclusion criteria, think of people who have other diseases where the medicine used in the study might make the patient sicker.

The autumn of 2014 proved to be a hectic time in both our personal and professional lives. Carrie had maintained her regular work schedule up to that point and was determined that she could maintain the pace. I got caught up in helping plan an emergency clinical research program to respond to the Ebola outbreak in West Africa. I went to Liberia twice in the month of October, but skipped a planning meeting in November to be with Carrie when she enrolled in the clinical trial.

While the NIH Clinical Center and, specifically, the NCI are great organizations, the bureaucracy of getting enrolled in a trial was somewhat overwhelming. Carrie quickly found that the requirements of participating in an intensive clinical trial, with intravenous dosing every other week, frequent scans, and lab work, among other things, would make it impossible for her to continue working as a counselor at the level she felt the position deserved. She submitted her retirement application and was able to stay at Crestwood until the end of January, when her protocol activities became more taxing.

The NCI staff did a great job explaining the various risks and benefits of the combination of the two agents, bevacizumab and dasatinib—neither of which were approved for her type of cancer. They made it clear that there was no way to know if any benefit would be seen, and that this small research study that enrolled approximately forty participants was to gain information to determine if it was worth pursuing this combination of agents in a larger study. These small trials were possible at the NCI, where clinician scientists could pursue questions that would not be commercially viable in studies funded by drug companies. Carrie was on board with the approach and went in with eyes wide open.

Such was Carrie's transition through the first relapse—an acceptance of the unexpected. These recollections remind me of how Carrie overcame the challenges of unexpected events that followed our arrival in Germany in 1990.

A New Life in Germany (1990–1993)

MARCH 31, 1977

... but I want so much more, to experience new people and places and do exciting things.

The assignment to Germany presented a tremendous opportunity for Carrie to fulfill her wanderlust desires. She did not hesitate to take advantage of it. While independence was never a problem for Carrie, our three years abroad allowed her to assert herself in ways she probably never envisioned as the twenty-year-old girl who wrote the passage above in her journal. Now at thirty-two, Carrie was thrown into an environment where she did not just survive on her own but thrived while effortlessly managing two energetic boys, as I departed for an unknown adventure of my own.

Four days after my arrival near the end of July, a strange event occurred in the Middle East—Iraq invaded Kuwait. I watched the news with curiosity, thinking that I was glad to be in Germany, defending the West from the Huns in the East. I gave little thought to how it would impact our family. I went about the next four weeks getting totally immersed in the new environment of Würzburg and the hospital where I worked. I volunteered to take weekend duty until my family arrived, a good way to make points with the staff, but also a way to learn how things worked at the facility. I was out of the temporary lodging within a few days and signed the lease for the townhouse in the Hexenbruch neighborhood of Höchberg. Hexenbruch was walking distance to the Fortress Marienberg, a castle built in the thirteenth century high on a hill overlooking Würzburg. As our car had not yet arrived, I bought a bicycle at the local post exchange and pedaled the five miles to and from the hospital. It was not too bad during the regular workday, but a bit of a pain when I was on-call at night and on weekends. Our furniture and car did show up before Carrie and the kids arrived. One of the reasons the Army delayed the travel of families was to make sure they did not get stranded without the comforts of furniture and transportation while the family's service member went out to the field.

Carrie and the kids arrived on Saturday morning, August 25, 1990. Carrie did an amazing job shepherding three-year-old Ben and five-year-old Dan on the overnight flight from Dulles. The boys were very much out of sorts coming through the customs checkpoint at the Frankfurt airport, and Carrie was exhausted. We drove the few short miles to the home of our good friends from Fort Lewis, Joe and Luralee Dettori, who now lived on the military installation in Frankfurt. Carrie and the kids crashed for a few hours before we got into the car and proceeded to our new home in Würzburg. Unlike Carrie's arrival in San Antonio in 1980, when I had picked out the place to live and Carrie had cried upon seeing it, everyone was happy with all aspects of the new home—Carrie loved it, the kids loved it, and I was thrilled they were with me and that we could go about being a family again. The place was a relatively modern townhouse with a small, enclosed yard. A playground was within walking distance, as well as an indoor swimming pool for year-round use. The sidewalks were full of kids about the same age as Danny and Ben. Of course, I really didn't pick out the house. Allyson, a fellow officer who was designated to help out with my arrival, had identified the place as she knew the home was being vacated by a departing colleague. Looking back, I probably did not say thank you enough to Allyson and her husband, Hal.

Notwithstanding the jet lag, the kids and Carrie got in a good sleep that first night, and we started exploring our environment on Sunday, taking in a service at the Leighton Barracks chapel, followed by a brunch at the officers' club. Carrie made mental notes of the opportunities available to herself and the kids within both the military installation and the chapel community. She also picked up brochures from the travel agency on the installation and went about planning potential summer vacations for 1991. Would we head to the beaches in Greece or Turkey?

Then there was the matter of getting the kids enrolled in school. Danny was old enough to enroll in kindergarten, and we needed to decide whether to enroll him in the American kindergarten or the local German kindergarten two blocks from our home. The DoD schools had an age cut off of July 1st, and Danny's birthday was June 29th. Carrie did not want Danny to be the youngest kid in his class. Moreover, the German kindergarten operated more like a pre-school than a kindergarten, and Carrie knew that the kids would benefit from playing with their German neighbors. As such, both boys were enrolled at St. Norbert's. The headmistress of the school spoke very little English, but the younger teachers were all gifted bilingual instructors and appreciated the opportunity to practice their English while helping the boys to learn German. The boys quickly mastered *spielen Deutsch*, basically speaking enough words so that they could play with their German friends.

Within the month, Carrie became acquainted with many of the neighborhood mothers who would drop their kids off at school and invite Carrie to one or another's homes for a cup of coffee. Many of these moms had an ulterior motive: They wanted the opportunity to practice their English more than to help Carrie learn German. Carrie did persevere and pick up some German phrases here and there, but she never came close to the boys' capacity to speak like a German. We spent our weekends exploring the forest down the street and wandering further in the other direction to visit the castle.

For Columbus Day weekend in early October, the Army pharmacists in Europe were invited to a small conference at a rather swanky hotel situated on Lake Eibsee at the foot of the Zugspitze, Germany's largest mountain. Everyone who had kids brought them along, so there were plenty of playmates for the kids. Carrie enjoyed the opportunity to get to know the spouses of the other pharmacists in Europe, especially as we would eventually congregate in the future for other "training" events. One of the family highlights during the trip was the opportunity to take a cogwheel train up the side of the Zugspitze.

We returned to Würzburg in time to turn on the news and listen to President Bush make an important announcement regarding the build-up of forces in Saudi Arabia in response to Saddam Hussein's occupation of Kuwait. The president had decided to send half of the forces stationed in Europe to Saudi Arabia. It did not take a degree in statistics to figure out the probability of deployment. Carrie was, of course, alarmed by this news, but I told her that chances were just as good that I would not get deployed as were the opposite—until the next day, when I received a call at work informing me of my pending deployment.

Going home after work and informing Carrie of the news was not a pleasant task, although she knew my cheery outlook from the prior day was just for show. She understood better than most people the random outcomes of flipping a coin and calling heads or tails. She was disappointed, of course, as there were so many things she wanted to do as a family, and now all that existed was uncertainty.

"When will you leave?"

"I don't know."

"How long will you be gone?"

"I don't know."

"How safe will you be?"

"I don't know."

You get the picture. We determined that the best thing that could happen would be that things came together sooner rather than later, but we thought that sooner would likely be after Christmas, as the pace for moving equipment to Saudi Arabia would dictate a later departure. Except, it was determined that I would be on the advance team to get things situated in Saudi Arabia before the equipment arrived.

It was the week before Christmas when word came down that I was to report to Stuttgart on December 24th. Not especially good news to bring home. Before going to bed that night, I made a short video, as was recommended, the one that would be played only if I did not come home. Seems like a morose thing to do, and it was. I deleted that tape as soon as I returned from the Gulf. We opened Christmas presents on the morning of the 24th with the kids before Carrie drove me to the hospital. The send-off was not happy, but it was not overly sad, as neither Carrie nor I wanted to be too emotional with the kids.

The next day, Carrie, with Dan and Ben in the backseat, gamely navigated her way to Frankfurt and the home of the Dettori family for Christmas dinner. Keep in mind that this was in an era when iPhones did not exist, nor did any sort of commercial GPS.

Carrie had step-by-step instructions written down from a phone call with Joe Dettori and confidently made her way to their home. It helped that reading signs in Germany was fairly easy as the alphabet is the same, but the speed of the autobahn and some of the different traffic laws that exist in Germany could be somewhat confusing to a new driver in the country. She and the boys enjoyed the opportunity to spend Christmas with old friends, who did their best to keep their minds off the uncertainties associated with my deployment.

Owen and Margaret arrived a few days after Christmas. Carrie, now with growing confidence in the navigation of roads in Germany, took the group to see several sights. The excursions included an overnight trip to Berchtesgaden, with a stop in Salzburg, Austria, and a brief foray into the former East Germany.

The trip to Berchtesgaden inspired Carrie to make reservations to take the boys back to Berchtesgaden in early March when they had a break from school, so that Danny could do a week of "ski kids," Ben could go to the daycare, and Carrie could relax and do some light shopping. In the intervening time in January and February, she stayed busy helping to organize a support group for others whose spouses were deployed, staying active in the chapel, and going to several social functions with our German neighbors. The kids continued to grow in their relationships with their German school friends and had frequent play dates.

On the return trip to Berchtesgaden with the boys in early March, Carrie had more travel opportunities than anticipated. Danny got smacked in the face with a ski and lost three of his front teeth. Carrie followed the ambulance across the border to Salzburg so Danny could get treatment—and found her way back to Berchtesgaden after dark. Even with the crazy way the week ended, Carrie enjoyed the opportunity to spend time away from the rumor mill of Würzburg and relax while the boys had fun.

Back in the Gulf, I found myself utilized not only as the director of pharmacy but also as the de facto hospital operations officer, coordinating various functions such as security, unit relocations, and interactions with higher headquarters. The circumstances were somewhat accidental, but I was glad to be in the position to help. Great life lessons were learned and friendships made. By the latter part of April, the hospital redeployed to Germany.

Carrie's persona during Desert Storm demonstrated that she was strong, confident, and independent. And she liked to travel! While I had the opportunity to do things during the war that would later mark me for a rare opportunity as a pharmacist to attend the Command and General Staff College back at Fort Leavenworth, followed by a PhD at OSU, Carrie was the real hero of our family. I was able to contribute to the effectiveness of our combat support hospital because I knew that Carrie was maintaining a clear head and doing similar things not only with our boys, but with a number of volunteer activities in the hospital and chapel communities. Neither of us was the one out in front, but we were instead behind the scenes, making things work in our respective endeavors.

Shortly after my return from Desert Storm, Margaret arrived from the States to allow us to take a short trip to Paris. We took the overnight train and arrived at 7 a.m. at the Gare du Nord station. We fueled up on good French coffee and pastries, purchased our subway passes, and set out to find our hotel within the French Officers Club. The common areas in the club were ornately decorated, but the rooms were just adequate. While we did get the opportunity to use the room for its intended purpose, our goal was to get out and see the sights and experience the city, and over the next three days, we did just that. Nonstop. We visited the Louvre, the d'Orsay, the Invalides, and the Rodin and Picasso museums. We toured Notre Dame Cathedral, assorted other churches, and the Arc de Triomphe. We floated down the Seine, took the elevator up the Eiffel Tower, walked along the Champs-Élysées and the streets of Montmartre, sat in streetside cafes, drank coffee in the morning and wine in the afternoon, and just enjoyed being with each other. We knew, again, that by divine intervention, the timing to do this at a point in our lives when we still had so much ahead of us was a rare opportunity, and we were thankful to experience it.

One afternoon, as we were enjoying a glass of wine at a streetside cafe, Carrie asked me what I thought about our trip.

"I think it's great, but there is still so much more to see. I wish we had more time."

Carrie looked across the aisle of closely arranged tables at a couple who appeared to be in their sixties and responded, "We can always come back when we're old and gray."

Ironically, while we were scheduled to return years later in June 2020, COVID got in the way and put the kibosh on that plan. Nevertheless, while we were gray in 2020, neither of us felt old.

Upon our return to Germany after seeing Paris, we did a few fun things with Margaret before she flew back to the States. We started "Volksmarching" as a family and found these local outings to be enjoyable opportunities to get to know the local area around Würzburg, get a little exercise, socialize with other people who joined us on the walks, and enjoy either a glass of wine or beer plus a bratwurst in the fest tent afterwards.

We took several weekend trips early in the summer, but the vacation in 1991 would not be a trip to the beaches of Greece or Turkey, as I had seen enough sand in Saudi Arabia to last a lifetime. In early August, we made our way north into Denmark and Norway. We first stopped at Legoland for a day and spent the night at a family youth hostel. The boys, fluent in German at that time, were confused that the other kids on the playground at the hostel did not respond to their Deutsch, while the parents, who could all speak multiple languages, told us that they were from Belgium and that the kids spoke Flemish. The kids played together despite the lack of any shared language. The next day, we made several stops before making our way to Hirtshals, where we would catch the five-hour ferry over to Kristiansand, Norway. The ferry was every bit as big as any ocean cruise ship, but the North Sea managed to make Carrie green in the gills.

We took off driving north towards fjord country, and we were not disappointed. The scenery was stunning. Around every turn was a view of a distant peak or of a rainbow waterfall. The kids in the backseat were not impressed. They were more caught up in the myriad of books and activities that Carrie had packed to keep them entertained for the boring parts of the drive, thus missing the spectacular views in Norway. Oh, well. We stopped along the way on a frequent basis to see touristy "stave" churches and to get our fill of the local lore. The kids finally became engaged when the tour guides told stories of gnomes and trolls. Over the course of the next two days, we went as far north as the glacier fields at Lom.

Our internal timetable told us it was time to head south as we had reservations in Oslo, where we stayed at a family youth hostel and spent two days exploring. Ben and Dan were a hit with the tour guide at the royal castle with their curious banter. We went to a Viking ship museum and visited sites used during the 1952 Winter Olympics. We also found parks along the way for the kids to get their fair share of play time during the trip.

We had similar experiences when we took the ferry back to Copenhagen. Very little of this adventure happened by accident. Carrie had consumed the travel guides and had plans A, B, and C available for every contingency. Even so, she frequently talked with the locals to verify that certain sights were worth the effort and adjusted plans accordingly. Both her planning and flexibility were admirable. This inborn skill Carrie had to orchestrate the adventures of our lives is a trait I now look back on with greater appreciation and respect.

When school started in the fall, Danny took the bus to the American school on Leighton Barracks for kindergarten, and Ben continued at St Norbert's. We took small trips through the fall of 1991 and enjoyed having Owen and Margaret along. Uncle Bill and Aunt Elma visited for the Christmas Holiday—a special time considering the craziness of what life had been like twelve short months before.

If 1991 was busy, 1992 would prove to be a year in hyperdrive. The war was over. The welcome mat was out. And people used it. In addition to two of my siblings and a spouse, family friends came to visit. We put lots of miles on the car, consumed a good deal of bratwurst, and enjoyed a few steins of beer. The highlight of the year was a trip to the UK with Owen and Margaret. Having Owen in the front passenger seat of our Taurus wagon as we drove on the "other" side of the road was somewhat unnerving. Regardless, seeing Stonehenge, visiting the Roman ruins in Bath, and visiting with Margaret's relatives in Wolverhampton and the London suburbs made for an enjoyable trip.

The stream of summer visitors continued with a group that Carrie had been looking forward to seeing: cousins Barb, Linda, Sissy, and Sissy's sons, Jeff and Jimmy. The Plank boys were old enough to entertain Dan and Ben so that the moms could sit down in the evening and enjoy a glass of wine without needing to over-supervise. Sissy planned an itinerary that would involve Carrie for part of the trip but also give her some free time away from their group. It was during that break for Carrie that we received a call from Uncle Bill telling us Margaret was in the hospital with breast cancer and that Owen was a basket case. This was startling news as they had only departed Germany the previous month. Carrie immediately made plans to return to the US, and I was able to take the cousin clan on the last leg of their tour.

Back in the States, Carrie quickly got Owen calmed down, but more importantly, intervened with the medical team to get the straight story on Margaret's prognosis. Carrie's direct approach was a bit of a shock to that team as they were used to dealing with senior citizens in Youngstown who took every word from the doctor as gospel truth. Carrie had them on their heels as she questioned everything. It soon became clear that after the mastectomy that Margaret had no positive nodes and that further chemotherapy was not warranted. She would go on to live into her ninety-sixth year.

After Carrie's return to Germany, we had time for one more summer adventure: a weekend trip to the North Sea beaches in Holland followed by a trip to Den Hague. By now, the boys were five and seven and observant of all things around them. Thankfully, they were pre-hormonal, as that beach, as with most every beach or outdoor swimming pool in Europe, was topless-optional for women. After getting ourselves comfortable in our beach location and looking around the environment, Danny posed this serious question to his mom and dad: "I understand where babies get their milk from, but why is it that some babies need so much more milk than others?"

Carrie and I did all we could to keep from busting out laughing. Carrie looked at me to see how I was going to respond.

"What an interesting observation. I have often wondered the same myself," I said.

My ribs remain sore to this day from Carrie's quick and sharp elbow.

Over the Columbus Day weekend in October, Carrie organized a three-day holiday to visit the mountainside town of Zermatt in

Switzerland, where a hike up to overlook the Matterhorn was a mandatory activity. Christmas 1992 brought along another visit from Owen and Margaret. This time, Carrie and I divided up the travel duties, with Carrie getting the better end of the bargain, taking her parents to Paris to see the Christmas lights.

The year 1993 would bring more visitors, travels, and changes. First was a trip to Berlin over Martin Luther King Day weekend, for which Carrie assigned me the planning. This was a sort of test, and though I didn't fail, my lodging choice was not ideal. I made up for it by getting us to a mix of tourist sites and finding fun things for the boys to do.

Later in the winter, my brother Ed and his fiancée Karen arrived for a memorable visit. As with many of our visitors, we first took them around Würzburg and that night, found a babysitter and introduced them to a German wine probe. The next day, we took them on an overnight trip to Neuschwanstein and Garmisch. On the way into Neuschwanstein, we got stuck in a notorious German traffic jam (*stau*) caused by a recent heavy snow that had most of the traffic headed to the nearby Tyrolean slopes for skiing. Going nowhere fast on the road, the kids began to feel the weight of their full bladders. As there were no gas stations nearby, Uncle Ed ran out into a frozen, snowy field with Dan and Ben following behind to christen the pure white sheet with the product of their relief. The kids thought it was a blast, and Uncle Ed became a rock star in their eyes. At some point during Ed's visit, I received a call from the Army pharmacy consultant back in DC telling me that I had been selected to attend Command and General Staff College at Fort Leavenworth. I told him that while it was a great honor, I had already completed the course by correspondence. He told me that it didn't matter, as this opportunity did not come around often for our specialty. I was informed that I would report to Fort Leavenworth before the end of June and follow-on that assignment with the PhD at OSU. I saluted the flag and said, "Yes, sir." In a lot of ways, going to Fort Leavenworth would make our transition back to the States substantially easier than moving directly to Columbus.

For Easter break, Carrie planned a trip to Italy. Of course, as Carrie planned this trip, the hotel in Venice looked out on the famous Rialto Bridge. We did the obligatory gondola ride and visited St. Mark's Cathedral and the Palace of the Doges. In Florence, we stood in lines for the Michelangelo Museum to see the statue of David. The boys made several friends, as there were busloads of American teenage school kids from various tour groups. Ben, who was a month shy of turning six, explained to a group of girls how to convert US dollars into Italian lira. The girls were most appreciative.

Our last big trip in Europe was the direct result of Carrie being able to make a nickel cry. In April of 1991, while still in Saudi Arabia, I was promoted to major, which brought my pay up to par with what a pharmacist in the civilian sector would make. During those next two years, Carrie did not change the budget book and socked away that extra money for a special trip she wanted to take before departing. In early June of 1993, we went to a family Club Med on Ibiza off the coast of Spain. To this day, I do not know how much this trip cost because Carrie managed the process without fanfare. At the Club, families were together for breakfast and dinner, but the kids were shepherded off for the remainder of the day. Carrie signed me up for snorkeling and sailing, but all she wanted to do was sit in the sun and read her books until our rendezvous for lunch.

Germany was a high-water mark for Carrie as a mother, life partner, volunteer, friend, cousin, and daughter. There were other times in Carrie's life where she would match that mark as an educator and counselor, and later as an advocate for patients with cancer. She would also have other periods of time where she would excel as a friend, parent, and life partner, but for those unforgettable three years, she was consistently tops. Carrie lived large in Germany, but not from the standpoint of someone who spent a lot of money. Her capacity to weather the unexpected storm of my deployment, along with careful planning, allowed us to have many great experiences, and we left Germany with several lifetimes' worth of great memories.

NOVEMBER 17, 1977

I've learned a lot about myself—my shortcomings and my ability to deal with problems I never thought I could handle. If I had it all to do over, there are a ton of things I'd do differently, but in doing them, I'd never learn from mistakes. I guess I gained most from messing up.

CHAPTER 5

The False Hope

"There were two exceptional responders . . . " from 39 participants.[2]

While 2015 did not begin with Carrie in remission, the treatment from the NCI clinical trial provided the foundation to get to that goal. However, unlike traditional chemotherapy, where a patient goes through a set number of cycles and is considered clear of disease, treatment with immunotherapy is substantially less uncertain when it comes to declaring an endpoint. Therefore, even when the cancer was determined to be in remission, the treatment continued—and would continue until either the side effects became intolerable or the cancer developed resistance to the treatment.

Shortly into the year, I departed for Liberia for the start of a large Ebola vaccine trial and arranged from afar a surprise retirement party for Carrie with the entire Crestwood staff and

---

2 Akosua Osei-Tutu et al., "A Phase I Dose Expansion Cohort Study of Dasatinib in Combination with Bevacizumab in Advanced Solid Tumors," *Journal of Clinical Oncology* 35 (2017),

neighborhood friends. Danny served as a sort of master of ceremonies at the event, which was held at a nice restaurant in Frederick. When I was out of the country, friends were available to drive Carrie into Bethesda for treatments that usually ended up being all-day affairs due to the number of activities required in a research study. Carrie made gradual progress as was anticipated with this type of treatment. As this was a research protocol, there were strict guidelines to ensure the patients remained relatively healthy for each dose. As such, there were narrow ranges allowed for the blood counts to vary. Whenever her red blood counts went down, the protocol stipulated an infusion of a unit of blood prior to treatment—a time-consuming process that had a separate set of risks. The most frequent problem with a blood transfusion is an event akin to an allergic reaction that can be managed with a shot of an antihistamine, but in severe cases, can require life-saving interventions. In the end, the blood transfusions were more of a nuisance than anything else.

Even with the challenges of getting accustomed to the new treatment, Carrie continued on her annual pilgrimage to New York with Sissy to see shows, and we were able to take trips to Texas, California, and the Pacific Northwest.

Early in 2016, Carrie was busy helping her mom, Margaret, move from Ohio to a retirement center located three miles from our neighborhood in Frederick. Carrie was also healthy enough to host both an engagement party for Ben and Renee at a local winery and a small wedding a week later, conducted by the judge Renee clerked for. The couple wanted to be legally married before departing for Ben's residency in Hawaii. They would have a big, elegant wedding later in 2018. Shortly after the private wedding, we were on our way to Phoenix with the newlyweds, Margaret, and my sister Diane for Ben's graduation from AT Still Osteopathic Medicine School in Mesa.

With all of this successful travel while on the study protocol, we thought the good times would continue to roll. But two weeks prior to a planned trip to Italy that summer with three other couples, Carrie woke up screaming of pain in her legs. I had yet to leave for work that day and ran upstairs to find the cause of the problem was sudden and substantial swelling in Carrie's legs—severe edema in medical terms. I called the study nurse, who said I could either take her to the local ER in Frederick or to the day clinic at the NIH. I opted for the NIH day clinic—a good call as it turned out that the leg swelling was the first sign of a major inflammatory response from an infection of unknown origin. Carrie quickly went from the clinic to an inpatient bed.

The availability of multiple medical disciplines within the NIH Clinical Center provided an umbrella of care that ensured both her cancer and this newfound infectious disease problem would be managed by experts. My colleagues from NIAID were the principal consultants in managing her care. These were physicians I interacted with from a research perspective, rather than in their clinical role as patient caregivers—a different paradigm.

I often found myself observing the distinction between the research and patient care roles and found a new appreciation for the clinical expertise of these physician/researchers. The attending infectious disease physician quickly ascertained that the problem was likely from an infected indwelling IV port, and as that was the primary route for administration of her immunotherapy, a series of diagnostic procedures were used to identify and treat the pathogen in order to keep this vital access route for treatment in place. Unfortunately, that exercise proved futile. Several antibiotics were used while waiting for the results from blood cultures. Scans were performed to try to identify the source of the infection. Over the course of ten days, nothing came back to identify the culprit. This was a frustrating time for everyone—the clinicians, Carrie, and me. Having exhausted all reasonable options, a decision was made to surgically remove the port. In many respects, it was a relief to move forward with the removal, as we were confident it would resolve the infection. But it proved to be a slow process.

Even after the removal of the port, Carrie continued to be a clinical challenge as the swelling from the inflammatory response did not resolve immediately. She needed an intense period of physical and occupational therapy to learn to walk again. That degree of physical limitation seems a stretch, but the impact of the infection was dramatic. The NIH was not set up for in-room overnight stays by family members, and I returned to Frederick every night around 10 p.m.

One night near the end of her hospitalization, Carrie called as I was driving off campus. She was in absolute distress, crying unintelligibly about something. I did a quick U-turn and hustled up to her room. She was sitting at the edge of her bed in tears.

"What happened?" I asked.

"It's my temperature. It went back up! I thought I was getting better, and now I'm getting worse!"

The nurse in the room with us was perplexed at Carrie's level of emotional response to the output from the temperature reading. The nurse commented, "I tried to explain there is a normal nocturnal variation in temperature, but she's not hearing any of it."

Knowing this was a nurse who had not cared for Carrie the previous ten days, I replied, "I think she is somewhat anxious as she is getting over a severe infection, and all of this is a new experience for her. By any chance, did the doctor include an as-needed order for lorazepam in the event that something like this might happen?"

Now understanding the situation better, the nurse responded, "I'll go look, but if there isn't, I'll get in contact with the on-call and get something ordered for her."

Carrie's situation was not particularly unusual for someone who had been an inpatient for more than ten days, as the potential for "hospitalitis" increases proportionally with length of stay. I was caught off guard as there were no earlier indications of stress. But sometimes, even the best of us let things get bottled up, and when the dam breaks, it creates a raging flood of emotional turmoil.

The next morning, a Sunday, I arrived to find a new infectious disease fellow sitting with Carrie and discussing the events of the previous night. I stood at the threshold of the door, somewhat like a fly on the wall, and did my best to listen to the conversation between Carrie and this relatively young physician. While I could not understand everything that was said, what I did appreciate was the calm demeanor of this doctor. I was most impressed with her bedside manner and capacity to engage Carrie. She asked probing questions and listened intently without talking or interrupting. She simply let Carrie get her frustrations off her chest, an underappreciated complement to the practice of medicine.

After discharge, Carrie remained on home IV antibiotics for another week and had visits from physical and occupational therapists to get back to full health. By mid-September, she was back to relatively good form. By October 2016, Carrie was feeling good enough to go to an OSU game. We stopped en route at a state park in Ohio and did some hiking, a tremendous accomplishment given that two months earlier, Carrie couldn't even walk. This was a great sign as Carrie, when healthy, loved her walks and found them invigorating. And to follow that up the following day with all of the walking involved in attending a football game with 105,000 of your closest friends also requires a certain amount of physical stamina. I relegated the incident of the infected port into the category of a speed bump on Carrie's way back to full health.

In January 2017, we took a trip to Hawaii, where Ben was doing his first year of an Army residency at Tripler Medical Center in Oahu. We spent the first four days with Ben and Renee in their thirty-eighth-floor apartment overlooking Waikiki Beach. We did things with the kids at night, as they were both busy with work, while we toured the island during the day. We took off for Maui by ourselves for a few days and had a great time exploring the Hanau trail before Ben and Renee flew over to join us for the weekend. With the kids, we woke up at zero dark thirty to go to the top of Haleakala to see the sun come up—a favorite tourist attraction. Ben, Renee, and I rode bikes several miles down to the bottom while Carrie traveled in the van with the tour company staff. Dining on Maui was fabulous. The opportunities to explore during the day, followed by slow dinners at night, provided a kaleidoscope of memories.

Later in 2017, it was obvious that improvements from the treatment were substantial, but so were some of the side effects. One of the drugs, belonging to a class of medicine known as kinase inhibitors, resulted in fluid retention in the lining around the lungs called a pleural effusion. This required a procedure for drainage and discontinuation of that part of the treatment. Carrie remained on the study with just the monoclonal antibody infusions, which had now been slowed down to once every three weeks. Even with this relatively minor adverse event, the clinical study team identified Carrie and one other research participant (not by name, of course) as exceptional responders to the study regimen. Carrie's encouraging response to treatment made me ask myself what the eventual fate was for the more than 90% of study participants who did not fall into the box of "exceptional responders." I didn't dwell on the topic at that time, but it was something I stored in the subconscious part of my brain, as the conscious part wanted to appreciate that Carrie was living an abundant life.

While I was away at a research meeting in November 2017, Carrie's mom, Margaret, had a stroke and was hospitalized for a short period of time. Carrie went about the business of making the necessary arrangements for her mom to get moved from her independent living apartment at Homewood into the memory care unit. Margaret, one of the kindest and gentlest people in the world, would never be the same. She became aphasic, meaning she lost the ability to make understandable words and sentences. Still, I always doubted the issue of "memory loss" as her eyes were always lively, and she had a warm smile and gleaming eyes when we showed her pictures from her many trips with us over the years.

The years 2017 through 2019 passed like a blur. Ben and Renee were properly married in Baltimore, we enjoyed the Outer Banks with brother Ed and Karen's relatives, took a fortieth wedding anniversary trip to the Inn at Little Washington, went to Wyoming to see college friends, toured Rocky Mountain National Park, went to NYC for more shows, and went to see the Buckeyes play TCU near Dallas.

Later in September and through the remainder of 2018, I got caught up again in an Ebola clinical research response, this time in the Democratic Republic of the Congo, which would eventually make me realize it was time to retire. For Carrie, though, a great adventure awaited her in late September, as she joined Sissy and two other ladies for a two-week trip around Italy. What a grand time they had traveling from Southern Italy to Florence and Venice.

Unfortunately, by early December, Danny's marriage to Rebecca had unraveled, as Danny's coaching life was more than she could endure. We continued to love Rebecca, but of course, focused our efforts on helping Danny get through the process.

The year 2019 continued to be good for Carrie, though I encountered a speed bump. While Carrie was in Italy in the fall of 2018, I had a prostate biopsy due to rising PSA scores, and the results came back positive. I was a little concerned, as my dad had died from a poorly managed case of prostate cancer. My brother

Mike, even with a surgically removed prostate, required multiple treatments to keep his cancer at bay. It was no small wonder that Carrie was adamant that I have the prostate removed, even though several other treatment modalities existed. In some respects, I think Carrie had a premonition that I needed to be healthy to take care of her at some unknown future date. Some sixth sense had her feeling uneasy. She wasn't overly anxious, but the term "insistent" would best describe Carrie's mindset about removing my prostate.

Fortunately, I had a great NCI surgeon, and the process involved a discussion with both Carrie and me about all aspects of the treatment options. The procedure took place in late April 2019 as part of a clinical treatment study involving a course of experimental vaccines for a few months leading up to the surgery.

I recovered in time for us to go to the Pacific Northwest for Ben's preventive medicine residency graduation at Madigan Army Medical Center and the conferral of his master's degree in public health from the University of Washington. During that visit, we were able to take the kids for a few days into the Canadian Rockies to see the spectacular sites in Banff and Jasper National Parks.

In September, Carrie traveled with me to a meeting in Merida, Spain. We flew into Lisbon, Portugal, where we rented a car and drove across the border. We were amazed by the restoration efforts of the Roman aqueduct, bridges, temple, and amphitheater in this relatively small city in the western part of Spain. While I was tied up in meetings, Carrie leisurely visited the UNESCO World Heritage sites. We returned to Lisbon after the meeting for a few days of touring. Not knowing that this would be our last big overseas trip, I now appreciate the quiet dinner we had on the far bank of the Tagus River, looking across at Lisbon. We ate fresh fish, drank our wine slowly, and meandered back to our hotel through the ancient streets. Life is full of memories that if we fully capture, as in a painting, we can always appreciate. I can still see that outdoor restaurant on a cobblestone street in the glow of the partial moon, with the sound of water slapping against the riverbank not far away, the aromas from the nearby restaurant kitchen, and the sight of Carrie across the table. We talked about everything and nothing. It seemed like time stood still on that evening. Maybe it did.

The year 2020 started full of promise of great things to come. I retired on February 29, 2020. We started my retirement with a full schedule of trips planned—a March trip to Florida to take in some baseball spring training games and a trip to Scotland to explore sites of our shared Scottish heritage. Trips to Paris and Geneva, Switzerland, were also planned later in the summer. What we did not plan on was the worldwide travel lockdown resulting from COVID. We did get to Florida before travel bans went into effect and enjoyed both the baseball and dining at some fun places in West Palm Beach. After one dinner, we went across the bridge to Palm Beach and drove up to the Breakers for an after-dinner drink, where we pretended to belong to the upper echelon who could afford such a place. We discussed the potential to come back another year for spring training and live large by spending one night at the Breakers.

After the travel bans went into effect, I was pulled back into a more regular consulting role at the NIH, serving as chair of the Division of AIDS' clinical scientific review committees that reviewed a portion of the COVID clinical research portfolio. Carrie continued to remain active, walking every morning, and while social interactions were limited, our bubble included our kids, who routinely joined us for dinner. As this was the year of our fortieth wedding anniversary in early July, we took a getaway trip to St. Michaels for a night and stayed at the Inn at Perry Cabin, the place where *The Wedding Crashers* was filmed. And while COVID precautions were in place, we still had a great dinner overlooking the finger of the Chesapeake that came into that sleepy little town.

Upon return from the Eastern Shore, things would take an unexpected turn. Even though Carrie was an exceptional responder to the NCI treatment regimen, our period of false hopes would come to an end. In retrospect, thinking it could go on forever was somewhat of a mirage. Regardless, it was somewhat like coming back to the States after three years of living the life of Riley overseas.

A Stateside Transition (1993–1997)

JULY 19, 1978

I think I'll enjoy working on my masters in the summer (and eventually a doctorate).

We returned from Germany and arrived in Dallas on June 24, 1993, for my sister Sue's wedding on the 26th. Recovery from jet lag was a bit tedious for all of us, but it was great to be back in the States and soon to be surrounded by our entire family, as Owen and Margaret were also invited to that wedding. Owen had retrieved our vehicle from the port in Baltimore and drove it to Dallas. But what to do when challenged with a day to kill while waiting on transportation in a hotel that did not have a swimming pool? The wedding ceremony was to be conducted at the chapel on the campus of Southern Methodist University, and we stayed at a nearby hotel. Carrie, being Carrie, researched a public pool within walking distance in University Park.

Carrie sent the boys and me on our merry way to that pool while she continued to make up for the jet lag and to get our clothes for the wedding organized, as they had been packed away tightly for the long air trip. The boys had a great time swimming, but were exhausted on the return trip to the hotel. *No problem*, I thought when I noticed a 7-Eleven a block from the hotel. *I'll get the boys a slurpy.* However, the boys had not been in a 7-Eleven over the three years living abroad, and the concept of a slurpy was foreign to them. People in the store gave us strange looks as the boys watched in amazement while the frozen concoction spilled forth from the machine.

Thankfully, cell phones were not as readily available at that time, or surely someone would have called the county social services to report the nut who kept his kids locked away in a closet and was only now exposing them to sunlight. On the telling of the story when we returned to the hotel, Carrie could not stop laughing and had great fun recounting the saga to the remainder of the arriving family—embellishing it, as was the Ague custom, with each rendition. The remainder of the wedding weekend was lots of fun reconnecting with family.

We departed for Kansas on the Sunday after the wedding, and by that night, we had signed into Fort Leavenworth. The next morning, the housing office at Fort Leavenworth assigned us quarters that were two blocks from where we had first lived in 1980. General MacArthur Elementary School was next door, which made the kids very happy. We took care of several administrative details that very long day, and as it became dark, the kids were amazed at a phenomenon that did not exist in Germany—fireflies. They got quite the kick out of chasing and catching these winged glowing insects.

Carrie was soon busy getting the kids enrolled in Cub Scouts, signing up for youth soccer and summer day camps, checking out the scene at the chapel, and visiting her old colleagues at Patton Junior High School. Even though there were no positions available, the principal was glad to get Carrie lined up to take over a long-term substitute role for a teacher getting ready to deliver a baby. Before that long-term assignment opened, Carrie became the go-to sub for every occasion and would end up working two to three days a week, which fit with her idea of how to leisurely get back into the paid workforce.

Regarding the social scene within the CGSC environment, Carrie had de facto legitimacy interacting with all the other spouses due to her three years of experience living on the installation in the early eighties. She quickly became the go-to source for where to shop for this or that, the best restaurant of a certain type, and the best routes to get to locations within Kansas City. Sometime during that fall, Carrie got the idea that adopting a kitten for the boys was a good idea. They enjoyed having a pet around the house and acquired some responsibilities for pet maintenance.

Throughout the fall, the kids continued to have lots of fun living in a neighborhood where every home had kids who would spill out onto the nearby playground at the school. The environment was similar to the one in McDonald where Carrie and I grew up during the '60s. The winter months brought about basketball season and the discovery of an emerging basketball capacity in Danny.

For spring break, we found ourselves on the road to Ohio to house hunt and to spend Easter with Owen and Margaret. We found the first house we would buy located on the northwest side of Columbus in the Hilliard School District. We made it back to McDonald on Saturday night, and we all went to Easter church service together before we departed back to Leavenworth—driving in the snow! It was one of those strange flukes that happen every so often in Northeastern Ohio. The school year quickly passed, and Carrie flew to Columbus to close on the house with an assist from

Owen, who met her at the airport. Before long, we were packed up and heading back east to Ohio.

The boys were now at the age where they could play the role of assistant navigator as Carrie and I each took one of the kids in a car. Carrie got the kids walkie-talkies so that we could coordinate pit stops along the way, and they thought it great fun to play their part in the move.

Carrie spent the summer of 1994 exploring part-time teaching opportunities and found a great fit with the Clintonville Academy, a private school not far from the OSU campus, where she would teach science to middle schoolers. At this point in her life, Carrie was not interested in pursuing her master's as she was now unsure which discipline in the field of education she wanted to pursue. Additionally, she rather enjoyed lesson planning for a new subject that she had not taught in the past, and at the same time, she was able to get home before the kids got off the bus. She also enjoyed the opportunity to interact with the teachers where the kids went to school. The boys immersed themselves in making new friends, playing fall soccer, and of course, following Ohio State football.

At OSU, I found myself quickly absorbed by the research group of Dev Pathak. Dev had a sort of "Yoda" persona, a Jedi Master always challenging his research team to identify the important questions in our field. More importantly, he understood my predicament of needing to finish the program in three years, but he also wanted to make sure that no corners were cut in getting me to the finish line. Dev set up an ambitious plan to make sure that I encountered the full range of required experience. This was a time not so much of learning but of learning to think—and apply. And more importantly, I learned from Dev to appreciate the fundamentals of outcomes research. Though I would never work in that field, those lessons would help me put Carrie's cancer journey into context.

Holidays in Columbus proved to be a great time, as it was an easy drive for either Owen or Margaret to come down, or for us to pack the kids in the car and go up to McDonald. However, the grandparents were always set on making sure the kids spent Christmas Eve in their own home—a tradition on their part that we came to appreciate as the stress of loading up presents to take back to McDonald would have made it difficult to keep Santa alive, even though both boys at this age, believed only for the sake of having an anchor to their past.

That first year in Columbus, Carrie and I entertained my fellow graduate school colleagues and faculty for a holiday get-together. As we were somewhat older than the other graduate school students, Carrie gravitated toward discussions with the junior faculty members and their spouses. It was an eye-opening experience for Carrie concerning the issues associated with the politics of tenure, and it made her realize that, even though she had the innate intelligence to obtain a doctoral degree, she was not sure that academia would provide a career pathway that she would find fulfilling.

The winter of 1994–95 held no big surprises. Carrie continued to enjoy her time at Clintonville Academy and would make several great friends on the faculty. One of her responsibilities that she took seriously was the organizing of the annual Science Fair. Given that the school was located in a recently gentrified neighborhood, it was not unusual to have many students whose parents were OSU faculty members, so Carrie would often rope them into serving as judges for the science fair. Carrie also cajoled me into participating, and I was always impressed with the creativity that the students displayed in their projects.

Carrie did not slow down during the summer of 1995. Two big projects—one for herself and one for Danny would consume the summer. Shortly after school let out, Carrie took off for Lake Erie and Ohio State's Stone Laboratory on a lagoon of South Bass

Island for a Natural Resources class entitled Great Lakes Education Workshop. Carrie was determined to be the best possible science teacher and found this course to fit an unmet need in her undergraduate education. While Carrie toiled away in class and on the water, the boys and I made an overnight trip to camp on a high cliff on the west side of the island. The one thing Carrie asked for on a phone call before we departed was to bring along a package of index cards to help her create her reference index for her project. I forgot the index cards in my haste to get the boys packed up and out the door. We met Carrie for dinner when we arrived, and while we thought she would be glad to see us, the absence of those cards spoiled her mood—substantially.

After being apart for a week, the boys (all three of us) got hugs, kisses, and grins.

"Have you guys been good for Dad this week?" she asked the boys.

"Yeah, Mom, of course! Dad's making pancakes for dinner! We didn't even know you could have pancakes for dinner!"

To me, she said, "I don't see the index cards."

"Index cards?"

"Yes, we talked about it when I called on Wednesday. I need those cards to create the bibliography for the research project we are doing!"

Dumb look in return.

Silence followed. The kids quietly looked between the two of us.

"I don't forget these kinds of things when you need something! You know what I really need? A secretary! Someone who can wait on my requests like you had working for you at the hospital in Germany!"

Carrie stewed at me and returned her attention to the kids. And I was a bit confused about Carrie's perception of a secretary.

First, I would never have asked the administrative assistant to get index cards. I would have gone to the storage room and picked them up myself. Second, I never thought of people working for me, always working with me. And last, if I were in her predicament without the cards, I would improvise and cut paper up into index card size and achieve the same result. But that wasn't the point. Carrie was disappointed because when she planned trips, she didn't forget things (or at least she claimed), and I had let her down. It was not the first time, nor would it be the last. Carrie would do just fine in the course, and like every other letdown, it was soon forgotten.

The second big activity was getting Danny ready to perform in a summer musical in Schindler Park in the German Village section of Columbus. Danny's music teacher at Norwich convinced Carrie to have Danny audition for a role in the Actors' Theatre of Columbus production of "The King and I." Danny played the role of Louis, the son of Anna, and had a few singing duets in the play. Carrie bought the soundtrack of the musical and had Danny listen to the tape as he went to bed so that he would subliminally memorize the words to the songs. It was a busy summer of shuttling Danny to and from rehearsals, and then to and from shows. The outdoor theater setting was perfect for that summer, and it helped the season fly by. Carrie and I took turns schlepping Danny, but on a few occasions, we left Ben with friends and went in together so we could have dinner by ourselves in one of the many German Village establishments while Danny was occupied.

The start of the 1995–96 school year would be relatively easy, as we were all settled into our respective routines. Football on Saturday afternoons and soccer on Sundays after church would be the schedule we worked around. The big event for Carrie in the winter of 1996 was her inaugural show trip to New York City. This would become her custom for the next twenty-four years until COVID shut down Broadway. This trip was scheduled for the Presidents' Day weekend as the vast majority of the ladies were teachers and were off work for the long weekend. In those early years, the moms went along: Anna Mae for Sissy and Linda, Elma for Barb, and Margaret for Carrie. A friend of Sissy's took care of the logistics. But much planning took place in deciding where to eat and what to do when not at a show, for example, which museums to visit. Carrie enjoyed every aspect and according to Sissy, was always agreeable to what the group would decide. Carrie would mark every calendar after 1996 with a red circle around President's Day, as that was her time. That was okay with us guys as we were more than capable of having sleepovers. Other kids would converge on our house, and we would watch every episode of the Star Wars trilogy, the Indiana Jones movies, and the Ghostbusters series. After the kids departed for college, Carrie used the trip to scout out shows she wanted the two of us to go see during the summer. The show trip weekend with the ladies was a great tradition for Carrie, and she made an entire group of friends that she would see twice a year, for the show trip and Sissy's holiday ornament party.

As the summer of 1996 approached, we finalized our plans to visit Atlanta. We'd received a Christmas card from Charlie and Kim Magee the year before, inviting anyone to stay with them for the Summer Olympics in Atlanta, and we took them up on the offer. At that time, online ticket sales were not yet available. There was a lottery process for which an application was available at the local library. Applicants identified ranked choices by type of sport they wanted to see and the days they wanted to see them. For track and field, the dates were listed, but not the specific track events that would be held on each date. We picked a variety of different sports, but were most interested in scheduling our visit when the finals of some of the track events were anticipated. As such, we selected dates towards the end of the Olympic schedule. And we were not disappointed.

We were lucky enough to have our track date coincide with the finals of the men's 200-meter dash when Michael Johnson shattered the world record. It was a long day sitting in that hot stadium, but well worth enduring many events of lesser interest. And our visit to Atlanta with Charlie and Kim was great. The summer concluded with me satisfactorily completing my general exams and transitioning to research on the dissertation.

As our Columbus years wound down, it was time to prepare for the pending move. The 1997 spring break for Clintonville Academy did not match dates with the Hilliard Schools, so the boys and I traveled to Maryland to get the lay of the land and begin exploring housing and school options. My follow-on assignment after completion of the PhD was to Fort Detrick in Frederick. The kids were of two minds regarding the pending move. On one side, they looked forward to something new, but on the other, they were a bit concerned as none of their friends were moving—and this was a very different phenomenon from what they experienced when leaving Fort Leavenworth. It was an indication to Carrie and me that future moves might only get more difficult. Carrie did homework on our behalf and lined up a real estate agent who spoke to us on several occasions to ensure that our needs were well understood. The boys and I went through several neighborhoods with the realtor, but more importantly, went to three different middle schools so that at least Danny would be comfortable with the potential setting.

And as spring bloomed, the pace of activities picked up even more. The boys were busy with spring sports. Additionally, Danny landed the role of Fagin in the Norwich Elementary production of Oliver. The music teacher at the school was most ambitious, and while the teacher initially thought of having one of the adult faculty play the role of Fagin, Danny's height and singing abilities convinced her to put Danny in that role. Danny was a smash as Fagin, and Carrie was a proud mom.

For Memorial Day weekend, Owen and Margaret came to Columbus and stayed with the boys while we went to Maryland for the definitive house-hunting trip. We went through several properties, but by the end of the weekend, we were down to two choices. Carrie thought we should put in a bid for the home that she liked, but it would be a tight squeeze for our budget (using the one-income rule). As the 1997 housing market in Frederick was unusually soft, we put in a low-ball offer. Shortly after returning to Ohio, the realtor called, informing us the offer was accepted.

Carrie should have been thrilled, but for some reason started to stress. Our Columbus home was sold quickly, and we had a closing date set with plans to be out of the house before the end of June. By the end of that week, Carrie was talking to a neighborhood friend, a lawyer, about the legal consequences of backing out of the offer. Not that she was asking from a legal representation standpoint, but just for general understanding. Carrie's concern was not so much the cost of the house, but the terms of the loan, as we were able to get a decent interest rate, but with an adjustable-rate mortgage. Carrie was terrified about the potential for the rates to go higher.

Later that night, she would have her first major meltdown while we were at the dinner table. There was no screaming or shouting, just a surreal emotional distress on her face. The boys and I looked at each other, not knowing what to make of the situation. Carrie departed the house and went for a drive. I was concerned that in her state of mind, she could easily get in an accident. She didn't. She returned within an hour, and while not in a bubbly mood, she had simmered down. We didn't ask her where she had been, and there were no apologies given—or requested. I didn't give this incident much thought at that time, as I knew the ordeal of moving was stressful. Carrie was at her best when things worked out perfectly, whereas the world of ambiguity was relatively normal from my upbringing.

We moved out of our house and spent the end of June and the month of July in McDonald, where I finished writing my dissertation, but still had time for some fun things with the kids. My research project on patient perceptions of alternative educational models in asthma treatment would later provide valuable insight into the realm of decision-making Carrie would encounter in her journey with cancer. My research helped me understand the nuances of patient perceptions of their disease, and that it was not a static function—it changes over time. And Carrie's perception of her cancer as well as her treatment would be somewhat consistent—until it wasn't.

JANUARY 31, 1977

Life is moving so fast. I've got to do all I can in the small amount of time I have, so I can leave my small, insignificant mark on the world of which I'm a part.

CHAPTER 6

The Reality of Recovery

The God I believe in does not send us the problem. He gives us the strength to cope with the problem.

– **Shirley Temple**

"Twenty-one of fifty-four participants achieved an objective response at six months . . . treatment continued until disease progression, unacceptable side effects, or withdrawal of consent . . .one treatment-related death was reported."[3]

It was after the trip to St. Michaels that Carrie returned to the NIH for a scan that would change the trajectory of her life. The results of that scan in July showed a tumor growing at the site above the psoas muscle and supporting nerves. The conclusion was that her cancer had become resistant to the immunotherapy regimen.

3 Vikki Makker et al., "Lenvatinib plus Pembrolizumab in Patients with Advanced Endometrial Cancer: An Interim Analysis of a Multicentre, Open-Label, Single-Arm, Phase 2 Trial," *Lancet Oncology* 20 (2019).

Carrie was not too shaken by the news. At least I don't think so, as during the COVID lockdowns, I could no longer accompany her to the appointments but hung out a few miles away doing work in the deserted NIAID office building. When I picked Carrie up after the appointment, she was somewhat composed for a few reasons. First, Carrie had beaten cancer twice and felt confident that she could do it again. Second, there was another study drug that was available, and she enrolled in that trial.

About that same time, Carrie got the idea that bike riding would be a fun activity to do together, and we went about getting her an e-bike. We started out taking short rides through the Francis Scott Key cemetery, as there was limited vehicular traffic and many people used the peaceful, historic location for walks or bike riding. With her confidence established, we spent the late summer and fall going several times to the C&O canal or over to Antietam and riding the roads along the battlefield. A vision emblazoned in my head is Carrie whizzing up a steep hill at Antietam on her e-bike and turning back, smiling and chiding me for not being able to keep up as I vigorously pedaled my regular bicycle.

In November, we spent a week at Ocean City, Maryland, while the wooden floors in our house were replaced. To mentally commit to this home improvement project, Carrie remained confident that she was going to beat cancer again. Every day we took long walks, appreciating the perspective of the scenery found in the late fall season compared to the summer beach. Carrie was usually tuckered out afterwards and took long afternoon naps while I got caught up on work projects.

About that same time, the NIH/NCI investigator informed Carrie that the new study drug was not demonstrating any effect on her tumor. The doctor did point out that a new combination therapy had recently been approved by the FDA for her specific cancer. As this was an approved therapy, it was easily accessible through any cancer treatment center. Were we concerned with the failure of the study drug? Not really. The prospects of the approved therapy, a combination of drugs similar to the immunotherapy regimen that worked for five years, provided us with optimism. The potential existed that the cancer would be susceptible to this new treatment.

Through discussions with the NCI investigator, we determined that Dr. Patrick Mansky at Frederick Health would be our best option, as Dr. O'Connor was now semi-retired. As the fall progressed, the tumor started to have an impact on Carrie's health. In a very transformative way, just her presence with me was special, and a tender goodnight kiss became considerably personal.

Such was the transition towards a tipping point.

Throughout the years, from 2008 to 2020, Carrie had not been defeated by cancer. She lived abundantly. In addition to working and being a positive force in the FCPS, she jumped into a number of volunteer activities after retiring in 2015. Carrie served one day a week as a driver for Meals on Wheels, helped with activities at the retirement center where her mom moved in early 2016, and was active in two cancer support groups, as well as church and community activities. We also went to concerts, shows, and speaker events locally, in Frederick and the greater DC region, and hiked nearby trails. Carrie maintained her routine of morning walks. She continued her annual weekend pilgrimage with the ladies to see shows in NYC. And there were several other trips and activities that Carrie undertook with Sissy and others, looking forward to each new adventure.

But the next treatment would change all of that.

After nearly thirteen years of successfully navigating her way through her initial cancer and the relapse of 2014, the relapse of 2020 resulted in Carrie's undoing. Not so much from the cancer itself, but from the accumulation of many factors: multiple treatments with their various short- and long-term effects, the emotional toll of dealing with both the cancer and the treatment side effects, and a gradual realization, though not verbalized, that getting through this was not going to end well. Carrie had pivoted towards a tipping point.

It was early December when Carrie had her first meeting with Dr. Patrick Mansky. As this was the first year of COVID precautions, we were all masked while sitting in that small exam room. Yet we could see in Dr. Mansky's eyes that he was a cerebral, caring, and compassionate oncologist when he thoroughly explained the benefits, and more importantly, the risks of the newly approved treatment regimen of a daily kinase inhibitor along with an every-three-week infusion of a monoclonal antibody. This was a similar yet different immunotherapy regimen than the one used in the clinical trial at the NCI. Regarding the benefits, Dr. Mansky made clear that this was a palliative treatment. That is, the treatment was not necessarily curative. Carrie looked to me for my thoughts on this option, and as it was consistent with the advice of Dr. Annunziata at the NCI, I nodded agreement.

Carrie started the first dose of the oral kinase inhibitor in late December of 2020 and the first infusion of the monoclonal antibody followed early in 2021. The lethargy started shortly after the initiation of the treatment. Carrie always liked her afternoon naps, but things were progressing to naps in the morning and extended afternoon naps. While not initially problematic, it was something that worsened almost imperceptibly until a point later when it became profound. In early February, I returned with Danny to Ohio for my mother's funeral, as Carrie was too sick to travel. Anxiety overwhelmed Carrie while she awaited our return, and she called several times wanting to know the status of our progress—a foretelling of things to come.

Carrie's initial gastrointestinal side effects were minimal, but by the end of February, those symptoms also became problematic. On Friday, February 26th, Carrie experienced worsening nausea and vomiting, followed by diarrhea. And the situation degenerated on Saturday, with my best attempts to keep her hydrated with oral electrolyte replacements. By the middle of the night, Sunday, the 28th, matters had deteriorated to the point that I called Dr. Mansky at home. He instructed me to take Carrie to the hospital. The staff physician considered admitting her to the intensive care unit (ICU) as her dehydration and electrolytes were wonky. Given the census of COVID patients in the ICU, a bed was found in the medical oncology ward, where, over the course of the next few days, her status improved. Endoscopy and colonoscopy procedures found nothing abnormal. Carrie was well enough to get discharged by Thursday, March 4th. After nearly five days in bed, she wanted to spend that relatively warm and sunny late winter day going to an early lunch and doing some light shopping. The early lunch worked out fine, but after less than an hour of shopping, she was sufficiently worn out that I needed to get her home and back into bed.

The fatigue would continue to be a problem. Carrie maintained a somewhat routine outpatient physical therapy program as microfractures on her spine were found on the most recent MRI. This finding was likely due to osteoporosis secondary to the high-dose steroids she received from her initial chemotherapy back in 2008. While many women gradually lose bone strength as they age, a side effect of high-dose steroid treatment can be a gradual weakening of bone function. When not at physical therapy, Carrie was wiped out and slept a good portion of the day. At about this time, she started coaching me on several things: a simple regimen of meals that I could make (and that she could tolerate), how to maintain the budget book, and the process for paying her mom's bills at the memory care unit. Why did I not interpret this switch of responsibility in household chores that Carrie coveted as her recognition that she was not going to survive? I was likely living in denial.

Friends from the neighborhood, church, and the various schools where Carrie worked, as well as Ben's mother-in-law and Sissy, frequently dropped off meals, reducing my culinary burden. As March turned into April, Carrie continued the treatment regimen, and the fatigue worsened. By the third week of April, I was sufficiently alarmed at the amount she slept and told her that she should contact Dr. Mansky. Carrie didn't want to bother him as she had a regularly scheduled appointment on April 22nd.

By Tuesday, the 20th, I could tell that Carrie was getting worse and called the oncology clinic, where they instructed me to bring her in. Dr. Mansky was not able to see her that day, but they drew a blood sample and administered a bag of IV solution with a steroid dose included. The clinic staff instructed her to return the next day for another IV replenishment. When we saw Dr. Mansky on Thursday, the 22nd, he took one look at Carrie and told me to take her to the ER for admission to the hospital. A lab test for thyroid-stimulating hormone had come back at a level of 150 (where normal is in the range of 0.5 to 5 mIU/L). Clearly, Carrie's lab result was off the chart and a cause for immediate concern. The medicines had destroyed the functioning of her thyroid gland.

The staff in the ER hastened to find Carrie an inpatient bed, something atypical in most hospitals, and we were upstairs early that afternoon. Carrie's confusion grew worse, and instead of continuing with fatigue, she grew into a state of hyper-agitation: up and down, tossing and turning, and pulling at IV lines. This continued nonstop through the night, and by about 5 or 6 in the morning, she finally fell asleep. I was relieved as I was not able to rest while her constant fidgeting and requests for help to go to the toilet and move IV poles kept me on the move. Except she wasn't just asleep—she had entered a coma. The day shift nurse was the first to recognize the situation and notified the hospitalist, who dutifully ordered an EEG. Nothing abnormal was found, and I sat there pondering what could go wrong next. Having watched Carrie's mental status slide precipitously during the last month, I wasn't shocked by the turn of events and had a basic understanding that the coma resulted from the severe hypothyroidism. I also knew that Dr. Mansky somehow foresaw this chain of events, and his direct order to go immediately to the hospital saved Carrie's life.

While sitting in that hospital room, I felt at times like I too was living outside my body, witnessing these strange events with Carrie that seemed beyond surreal. In his book, *The Body Keeps the Score*, Bessel van der Kolk describes these out-of-body dissociation experiences as a defense mechanism that we subconsciously take when confronted with trauma. It would appear that I was traumatized by witnessing what Carrie was going through. And things only got worse.

Late in the afternoon, atrial fibrillation started setting off alarms and causing considerable activity amongst the staff. The ICU team was called in, and I was told that they were going to intubate her and take her down to the ICU. I had a well-reasoned curiosity in watching the nurses take care of Carrie, as I knew I would eventually need to learn these skills, but I had no stomach to be in the room during her intubation. While the room became crowded with the ICU team, I cleared out her stuff and took what was not going to be needed out to our car. I returned to the ICU to find Carrie still in a coma, but not with an endotracheal tube. The ICU doctor explained that after I left, he re-evaluated the situation. As Carrie was breathing on her own, he determined that intubation was not necessary. A small blessing. Another plus (for me) was that family members could not spend the night in the patient's room in the ICU, and I was out of the hospital by 10 p.m. and on my way home. Even though my head was spinning, the previous long night in the hospital left me exhausted, and I fell asleep immediately.

During that long day, Friday the 23rd, I did not contact either of the boys or Sissy. We had on our calendar for that day a retirement party that Sissy was hosting for Mike, and I didn't want Carrie's situation to be a damper on that event. And I really didn't have enough information to communicate. The next morning, Saturday, I sent all of them a text message with a summary of Carrie's hospitalization and asked them to meet at Ben's house, three blocks away from the hospital. I was able to give everyone the update in one setting, thereby reducing the potential problems associated with giving different stories to each person. They were all concerned about Carrie's condition and understood that it was just going to be a matter of wait and see.

Fortunately, Carrie's eyes started fluttering late Sunday, and on Monday, she was coherent but substantially confused. On Tuesday, she was transferred up to a medical telemetry ward where her heart could be monitored around the clock. The prolonged hospitalization resulted in a few delirious episodes where she would have conversations with people who were not in the room—probably a consequence of spending three days in a coma, where she was surrounded by external stimuli. By Friday, she was climbing the walls to get out of the hospital, but the speech pathologist was an obstacle to her discharge as Carrie failed a "swallow" test, which was challenging given that she had her nasogastric tube for feeding removed earlier that day.

By Saturday, May 1st, Carrie asked me to get her changed into street clothes so that she could go for a wheelchair ride around the hallways. Once outside the room, she asked if we could make a run for it—which was a bit comical as she still had a few IV lines attached.

"Where's the car?"

"In the parking deck."

"Do you think anyone would notice me leaving the floor in this wheelchair?"

"Probably not, but we don't need to make a run for it. This isn't the Hotel California. You just need to let the nurse know you want to check out Against Medical Advice."

"And that's all there is?"

"I think so, but I can't say I have ever witnessed the process."

"Okay, let's find the nurse and tell her I want to leave."

The nurse was a bit nervous and contacted the hospitalist, who was sympathetic to Carrie's plight. The hospitalist, for some reason, could not countermand the speech pathologist's recommendation to remain hospitalized, but also did not object to Carrie leaving Against Medical Advice (AMA). We were out of the hospital by noon that day and immediately drove down the street to Ben's house. Ben ordered a pizza, and Carrie had no problems swallowing. She felt it was the best food she'd had in months, the statement she would often make when under duress, even with the last thing she ever ate. Feeling like I was transporting a person free from prison, we went home, where Carrie immediately went upstairs and fell asleep. This time, I knew it was just the sleep of exhaustion from being in the hospital. Carrie slept so soundly that she didn't realize she had wet the bed early in the evening. After directing her into the shower, I changed the bed. Now clean and dry, she climbed into the fresh sheets and conked out again until the morning.

The Frederick Health home care team was wonderful after the discharge and provided abundant physical and occupational therapy, as well as great support from the palliative care nurse. Carrie's next medical challenge, though, was to address the microfractures that had been discovered in her spine. Any travel in a vehicle was painful, as every bump she encountered resulted in shocks of pain. We were able to get in to see the neurosurgeon on short notice, and a kyphoplasty procedure was scheduled. This was a minimally invasive procedure used to treat vertebral compression fractures by inflating a balloon to restore bone height and injecting bone cement into the vertebral body.

Carrie was adamant about the resolution of the spine so she could make it to the last of the graduation parties for the Pierson clan. Karen, our sister-in-law, hosted these events for her five children and eighteen nephews and nieces. These parties were legendary for their size and the ability to catch up with extended family. Carrie recovered and made that four-hour trip in reasonable shape. We both enjoyed the opportunity to reconnect after the challenges that COVID posed in attending family events.

We spent the remainder of the summer getting our house reconfigured to facilitate the support of Carrie's growing mobility issues. An additional handrail was added to the opposite side of the staircase, we added assist rails to the toilets, and a rail was added outside our garage door to help Carrie enter the house. Carrie was not yet using a walker but did use a cane and religiously attended physical therapy sessions for the remainder of the summer. She also went through acupuncture treatments to keep pain at bay.

The summer continued into August, and Carrie's last treatment had been in late April. The tumor over the psoas muscle continued to grow, and pain management became a problem. Carrie was probably too slow in reporting the pain, but when she did, Dr. Mansky was thorough in making sure it came under control quickly. Dr. Mansky also recognized that to address the source of the pain—the tumor—additional treatment would be needed. CyberKnife radiation treatments took place during the month of

September, and Carrie resumed the monoclonal antibody treatments. Unlike conventional radiation techniques traditionally used to treat certain types of cancer, the CyberKnife machine delivers a high dose of radiation with fewer treatments than the standard method.

Over the fall and into the winter, Carrie continued with the immunotherapy, which had been changed to an every-six-week infusion by this point. Her fatigue was not as bothersome, but she was still far from normal energy. Her left leg gradually weakened, as the September radiation treatment, combined with a round of radiation from back in 2014, had a cumulative effect.

In December, my brother Ed and his wife, Karen, visited Frederick. Karen, a whirling dervish of energy, used the opportunity to do the normal Christmas decorating that Carrie always enjoyed. While Karen was doing her thing, Ed and I went for a hike on a trail in the Monocacy Battlefield, followed by a pint at a local brewery along the Carroll Creek promenade in Frederick. It was a relatively warm December day, and we sat outside where I confided to Ed about my concerns regarding Carrie's prospects. I had spent a good deal of time researching papers on "PubMed" about the outcomes associated with her current treatment, as well as the statistics associated with survival with a third return of cancer. I told none of this to Carrie. While sitting in the pleasant December sun with Ed, I revealed the findings of the literature review—that it appeared Carrie would likely not survive beyond eighteen to twenty-four months. After Carrie's death, I would learn that Carrie knew in her heart that her days were numbered.

Carrie coached me through the preparation of Christmas dinner for 2021. Carrie normally took great pride in the preparation of the kind of dinner her Grandma Ague would make, going to a farm butcher rather than the grocery store to procure just the right kind of filet of beef to roast, using the juice from the beef to make gravy and Yorkshire pudding, and a spread of vegetables—plus crabcakes when Renee, the pescetarian, joined our clan. The only thing left out of the normal spread was the cookies. Baking was a bridge too far for my limited skills around the kitchen. Carrie found a comfortable chair in the kitchen with a pillow behind to prop up her back and patiently walked me through the preparation of the meal, including the setting of the table with all the Christmas dishes accumulated through the years. Most of the things were from our three-year German odyssey, where shopping for Christmas items was a favorite activity for Carrie. This would be the last year for Carrie to take even a small part in the preparation of the Christmas meal.

December rolled into January, and the winter of 2022 proved somewhat quiet and uneventful as Carrie continued her monoclonal antibody treatments and visits to the physical therapist and acupuncturist. She somehow remained active in her book clubs and church activities through Zoom. Sissy was a frequent visitor who helped maintain Carrie's good cheer. In early March, we were able to go to Ohio for a family wedding. At the wedding, held in the Arcade at the Hyatt Regency in downtown Cleveland, Carrie could only last through the ceremony and the dinner before I helped her back up to the room to get comfortable. I returned to the festivities, and unfortunately, Carrie missed out on her last opportunity to be part of the Pierson family pictures.

A few weeks after the wedding, we took our last trip of any significance, a few days in a cabin near Gatlinburg, Tennessee. On the way down, we stopped to have dinner with a good friend, Nancy Bil Leslie, from our Columbus days. We got caught up on the status of our respective families, and towards the end of our conversation, Nancy Bil insisted that we must come back next year, 2023. Carrie was hesitant, but gave an awkward smile and stated simply, "Of course, I am going to do my best to be here next year."

My sister Cathy had always talked up Gatlinburg as a great place to see—and it was. Our cabin was far enough outside Gatlinburg that we were not caught up in the surprisingly busy traffic of that town. I searched the vacation rental spots long and hard to find a spot with very few stairs, as those now represented a major hurdle for Carrie. I gained a new appreciation for issues associated with individuals facing mobility challenges. Even so, Carrie was able to get out of the car at the various scenic stops in the park and even took a very short hike with the support of her cane. Cathy recommended some great places to dine, and we took full advantage of that advice. Even so, it was difficult for Carrie to fully enjoy the week.

The months of April and May remained somewhat uneventful, but Carrie's mobility continued to deteriorate due to the progressive nature of the radiation injury. Dr. Mansky recommended that Carrie seek a neurology consult for the pain running down her left side and into her leg, as pain management was getting more problematic. Carrie went through an initial visit with the neurologist in early June, who scheduled a nerve-conduction test for a date in July, which would become a moot point as circumstances would prove.

I could see that things were not going to improve for Carrie, but I thought that the descent along her terminal slope would be a gradual decline.

Unfortunately, my expectations soon proved wrong.

These events reminded me of times when marriage was challenging, but not insurmountable. As described earlier, we had our ups and downs. And the strange thing is that we never discussed our down times. Carrie would just get over whatever it was that was bothering her, and I would make mental notes to avoid repeating whatever might have triggered an episode. However, again, due to limitations imposed on us carriers of the XY chromosome, figuring out where I went wrong is not always obvious.

And now, facing a medical and not an emotional challenge, the rational side of my brain was telling me that things would not improve, and the emotional side wanted Carrie to survive. But I was challenged in adequately communicating either of these thought processes.

FEBRUARY 1, 1977

Today was one of those days. Hopefully, tomorrow will be better in that sense.

Part Two

The Power of Struggling

Time moves slowly but passes quickly.

– Alice Walker

Gone from My Sight

I am standing upon the seashore. A ship at my side,
spreads her white sails to the morning breeze and starts
for the blue ocean. She is an object of beauty and strength.
I stand and watch her until at length she hangs like a speck
of white cloud just where the sea and sky come to mingle with each other.
Then, someone at my side says; "There, she is gone."
"Gone where?"
Gone from my sight. That is all. She is just as large in mast
and hull and spar as she was when she left my side.
And, she is just as able to bear her load of living freight to her destined port.
Her diminished size is in me, not in her.
And just at the moment when someone at my side says, "There, she is gone,"
there are other eyes watching her coming,
and other voices ready to take up the glad shout; "Here she comes!"
And that is dying.

– Author Unknown[4]

4 The origin of this poem cannot be verified. While it often attributed to respected American author, poet, and clergyman Henry Van Dyke, there is no record of him writing this poem. It was most likely written by Rev. Luther F. Beecher (1813–1903), a relative of Harriet Beecher Stowe. The poem was found in Carrie's nightstand two months after her death.

CHAPTER 7

Beyond the Tipping Point

MAY 1, 1977

Well, the end is near . . .

On the morning of Wednesday, June 8, 2022, while I was finishing up my shower in the basement after a short run, I heard Carrie screaming from upstairs. I ran to find her on the bathroom floor, howling in pain. Her leg had given way while she was standing at the sink, and she knew immediately that she had fractured her shoulder hitting the floor. I called 9-1-1, and before the ambulance arrived, a neighbor from down the street, a retired first responder who often listened to the emergency scanner, was at our door asking where he should direct the ambulance crew upon arrival. What a timely assist. Noting Carrie's extreme pain, the ambulance team was careful loading Carrie into the stretcher to get her downstairs. There was no way I could have done that by myself. I followed behind in my car. The drive took only minutes, and along the way, I somehow knew that this might be the beginning of the end—and I was not ready for it.

Unfortunately, the ER was a zoo that day, and Carrie waited an interminably long time to get into a bay to see a PA. An X-ray confirmed the shoulder fracture, and this particular PA somehow looked at Carrie as a patient with a shoulder fracture—and not at the proximal cause of the fall, a left leg that had given way due to a radiation injury that slowly destroyed the nerve function. Moreover, the PA failed to appreciate the looming inflammatory cascade that was slowly festering within Carrie's body from the super-charged immune response facilitated by the monoclonal antibody—a perfect storm. As the PA proceeded to provide instructions for Carrie to return home and do her best to rest in a recliner chair until she healed, the nurse in the bay gently recommended that the PA consider hospitalization. I was thinking to myself, *Finally, someone who can see that Carrie requires more medical attention than I can provide at home.* However, the PA was unmoved by the recommendation. I was somewhat stunned but remained silent. By all objective measures, the PA was correct in her assessment. However, sometimes healthcare providers need to rely more on soft skills and be able to look at the long-term implications of their actions. Unfortunately, that is a challenging undertaking for any provider in an emergency department.

Carrie was wheeled out to my car and loaded with the help of the ER staff. When we returned home, our good friend and church visitation pastor, Linda Warehime, and her husband, Bill, met us at the house and helped unload Carrie. Bill and I did our best to get her up those few steps. It was torture for Carrie as every small movement or jolt caused pain to radiate through the entire left side of her body. When we finally did get Carrie into the recliner chair, she was far from comfortable.

Finding a bedside commode to set up next to the recliner was easy. Unfortunately, getting Carrie out of the chair and onto the commode was a challenging task and extremely painful. The next morning, a home health nurse showed up for an assessment and determined that if Carrie was going to make any progress, she would need regular visits from physical therapy, occupational therapy, and a nursing aide. The aide showed up later that day and was a bit surprised that Carrie was not in the hospital. The aide proceeded to do her best to help clean Carrie up and make her more comfortable. We went about getting disposable undergarments as it became clear that getting Carrie transferred to the bedside commode was not going to work. The next day, Kate Ague, a second cousin, stopped by to provide some help. Kate had recently finished nursing school and was going through orientation at the University of Maryland hospital. Kate was a big help in further educating me on caregiving duties.

While during previous hospitalizations, I had helped Carrie move her IV pole to and from the toilet, this was an entirely new frontier, as even getting to the bedside commode was a bridge too far. Carrie found it too painful when I attempted to get her to stand and pivot onto the commode. Now it was a matter of helping to change out the Depends—a necessary task where my transformation into a dedicated caregiver started in earnest. Everything prior to this point was easy. The process required a certain amount of emotional detachment. I was not sure if I was ready, but sometimes you need to step up and march into the breach regardless of whether you know what you're doing (or not).

Carrie's condition continued to deteriorate through Friday and into Saturday. She just didn't look good. Late Saturday afternoon, a friend delivered a pulse-oximeter, and the result was as I feared—an oxygenation level below 90, a clear indicator that medical intervention was required. When the ambulance arrived, Carrie was unsure if she wanted to go back to the ER, as her experience from earlier in the week was so terrible. The ambulance crew and I talked her into taking the trip as we all thought hospitalization was warranted. And this time, even though it was a Saturday night in the ER, Carrie was seen by a physician and transferred to an inpatient room in relatively short order. This was such a different experience from a few days earlier, and we were both relieved—emotionally, physically, in every way you can think.

Carrie could finally get comfortable in the hospital bed and, even with frequent vital sign checks from the nurses, had no problems falling back to sleep after each check-in. During this hospitalization, as with all other non-ICU hospitalizations in Frederick, I stayed the night with Carrie. Compared to sleeping in the field in the Army, the recliner chair in the hospital was quite comfortable.

Carrie, though her oxygenation level was low, had nonspecific symptoms. The GI effects had yet to emerge, and her hydration status was adequate, so the hospitalists ran a few tests and determined by June 17th that she was not so sick that she should stay in the hospital, but too sick to go home. Carrie accepted the recommendation for discharge to a convalescent center due to the availability of more nursing care than I could provide, along with intensive physical and occupational therapy. Fortunately, this was about a mile from our home. Another plus (for me) was that the facility had a policy against overnight visitors. I was able to get some good nights of sleep. Even though I slept well in the hospital, nothing compares to sleeping at home in one's bed. In the convalescent center, where there were very few external stimuli, such as beeping monitors, and where frequent vital signs were not part of the routine, Carrie slept better and was not bothered that I was not at her side.

Carrie lasted in the convalescent center four days when they determined that she needed to be brought into the ER—on the evening of her birthday. This time, the ER determined she just needed to get a few bags of IV hydration and sent her back to the convalescent center in the morning. What a long night that was for all of us. Carrie returned to the convalescent center through a patient transport service and continued to work with the physical and occupational therapy teams. She did her best learning the technique for a slide board transfer from the bed to a wheelchair, but even that task required at least two people to assist her. Attempts to get her to stand with a railing assist were challenging as she had lost all sense of balance due to the left-side injuries. And with each day spent in bed, her entire body, and especially the left side, weakened. What a conundrum.

By June 28th, the staff at the convalescent center again thought that her nursing care needs exceeded their capacity and called the ambulance to bring her to the hospital. I had gone with Danny to an Orioles game that evening. Carrie thought it would be a nice birthday present for Danny and that she could get by for a few hours without me. The convalescent center called me somewhere in the middle of the game about the transfer. Danny and I hurried back from Baltimore, and I caught up with Carrie in the ER. Carrie presented as a medical mystery as the inflammatory cascade building up in her body did not fully manifest itself, but she was dehydrated and in need of electrolyte replacements. A full range of tests was conducted to determine the cause, but by July 3rd, no one could quite put their finger on the problem. Carrie went back to the convalescent center. It was far from ideal, but she was too sick to go home and not sick enough to stay in the hospital. And whatever was brewing inside her had not yet revealed the extent of how bad things would become.

Throughout this time, Carrie was also planning a baby shower for the pending arrival of our grandchild and had me out running errands to the caterer to make sure that things would work out just right for the event scheduled on July 9th. Family from many states were due to converge upon Frederick. We made plans with the convalescent center to get Carrie a day pass to attend the shower with the help of their wheelchair transport van. Unfortunately, Carrie's condition again deteriorated, and the true nature of her illness was becoming abundantly clear. She had lost all control of her bowels, and the nursing team was stretched with changing out her bed every few hours, even with my help at every step. Back to the ER and admission to the hospital.

Fortunately, my sister-in-law Karen arrived that evening and told Carrie that she would fill her role as co-host at the shower. Sissy came to the rescue and sat with Carrie at the hospital on an iPhone video call with Karen, who was at the shower, so Carrie could appreciate the fruit of her successful plan.

By Monday morning, the GI consultant was on top of things, running both an endoscopy and colonoscopy while obtaining biopsies along the way. The GI doctor thought that a fistula had developed between Carrie's large intestine and her vaginal tract as it appeared that fluid was leaking from everywhere. Intensive steroid treatments were started along with other medicines to slow down what was finally diagnosed as severe immune-mediated colitis. Several different treatments were administered, similar to throwing spaghetti against the wall, but nothing stuck. Throughout the hospitalization, Carrie, though not verbally stating it, was feeling humiliated by the frequent bed changes required and the lack of control she had over her own bodily functions. Her eyes appeared to have the look of someone held hostage with no way to negotiate her way out of this predicament.

As the output was mostly watery, the nursing staff inserted a rectal catheter. But even these devices were prone to leaking, and at times, the volume of discharge would overwhelm the tubing. I helped to the point where I could instruct staff on some shifts who were unfamiliar with how to insert and maintain the tubing. Carrie would apologize for being "that patient" every time she needed to have the device changed. I don't know if I could ever go through what she endured.

By the end of July, surgical options were presented, and while some members of the medical and oncology teams wanted to continue onto other treatments, Ingrid, the nurse practitioner (NP) on the team, had the good sense to listen to Carrie and advocate for what Carrie wanted—to stop the colitis as soon as possible. If the surgical option with an ostomy would stop the colitis, Carrie was willing to endure it. The NP also explained that getting the surgery was a function of timing, as it would be desirable to get scheduled with the best surgeon available, and we were fortunate that Dr. Naderge Pierre was available to perform a reversible ileostomy.

Carrie did well with the surgery, and I went through intensive training with the ostomy team on how to care for the site and the changing of the appliance. Carrie was still far from ready for discharge, as throughout the long hospitalization and loss of fluids, her nutritional and metabolic status required that she go onto hyperalimentation feeding—feeding through a peripherally inserted central catheter, or PICC line.

While recuperating, Carrie and I planned a combined welcome-home and promotion party for Ben. Ben returned in late July from deployment to Kuwait and was promoted from captain to major during the time he was away. Again, Sissy came and sat with Carrie while I went to the event and acted as host for a few hours before passing the baton onto Danny so that I could return and relieve Sissy.

Throughout the hospitalization, Carrie's separation anxiety continued to grow, and I rarely left her room. I usually woke up before 6 a.m. and would go the few miles back to our house, shower and eat, and be back in the hospital before Carrie awoke. If I were not nearby, Carrie would either be reaching for her cell phone to call to find out where I was and when I would be back, or if she could not find her phone, she would be hitting the call button, asking the nursing staff to find it for her. It was a troubling development in a person who had been so independent for the previous forty-two years of our marriage. This was such a different person from the one who thrived when I was away at Desert Storm, stationed in Korea, or traveling to Africa to support Ebola clinical research. When Carrie called under duress, I did my best to get to her side as soon as possible and reassure her that I was never far away.

By mid-August, Carrie was no longer sick enough to require hospitalization. But the question remained: discharge to the convalescent facility or go home. For Carrie's emotional well-being, we determined it best to come home and to hire a home health aide.

We were also fortunate that my sister Diane came out the day before Carrie's discharge. Diane was able to meet the team from the home medical supply company and directed the placement of the bed and the various pieces of equipment. Diane had been a nurse for twenty years before going to medical school and becoming a pathologist—but she never forgot her nursing skills.

Sissy arranged for a portable wheelchair ramp to be available at our house before Carrie returned home. And as anticipated, Carrie slept soundly those first few nights at home, probably due to exhaustion. The next day, Frederick Health sent in their team of a palliative care nurse, a wound care nurse, a physical therapist, an occupational therapist, and a home health aide. I remain amazed at just how much muscle strength is lost when a patient is confined to bed for a two-month period. Getting Carrie moving now that her left arm was healing was going to be a major challenge.

The wound care nurse, as well as the physical and occupational therapy team, were wonderful. All along, I remained the only person who maintained the ostomy care, except for when the wound care nurse visited and helped me go through the paces to ensure I was doing everything correctly. During those first few weeks, Carrie continued to receive hyperalimentation delivered through a home IV service company. She made slow but steady progress with PT and OT as her shoulder continued to recover. Even at discharge from the hospital in August, the entire left side of her body was black and blue and would eventually clear up by October.

I procured a simple baby monitor system so that I could sleep upstairs and listen if Carrie needed me for anything. We always shared a tender goodnight kiss before I trudged up to bed to read for a few minutes before falling asleep, exhausted. Most nights went by peacefully for me, although Carrie slept fitfully. She only called me when the ostomy appliance failed for one reason or another. Those were high anxiety moments for Carrie. I developed a system to always have a full replacement set ready for application, but the process of removal and reapplication could be tedious, depending on the extent of the leak. I generally talked to Carrie in an even-keeled manner to limit the potential for further anxiety. I pointed out that the spill was not that bad, and I engaged her in helping by holding a towel in place or performing some other task that would keep her occupied while I dug into the ready bag to change out the components of the ostomy collection unit.

In hindsight, I realize that my caregiver role ended up causing me to become emotionally detached—something I now regret, as there are times I could have been more consoling rather than assuming the clinical helper role. And it was at times like this when Carrie was scared that she also needed someone who could give her a hug and tell her everything would be okay. However, it was nearly impossible to give her a proper hug, given the way the bed and tubing were set up. And while I did my best to allay her fears, I could not knowingly tell her that everything was going to be okay.

In mid-August, Ben and Renee took a pre-birth trip to spend the night in Bethesda and have a nice dinner. The baby was not due until mid-to-late September. The trip turned out to be a nightmare for Renee as she developed symptoms of preeclampsia. Ben rushed her back to Frederick Health, where she stayed for less than a day before a decision was made to fly her out to Johns Hopkins in Baltimore for high-risk care. Renee was eventually diagnosed with posterior reversible encephalopathy syndrome (PRES), which, if not managed carefully, could result in the death of both the mother and child.

A C-section was immediately scheduled as the primary means to stop Renee's body from generating the dangerous feedback loop, and baby Fern came into the world on August 21st. The birth was premature, but the baby was healthy. However, Renee was far from out of the woods and required intensive care for a few days to get her blood pressure under control. Fortunately, she gradually improved. Carrie and I were both concerned and a bit bothered that there was nothing we could physically do to help, although we did activate the prayer chain at Brook Hill. It took several days before Renee was out of the woods and ready for discharge.

One of the first stops for Ben and Renee upon their return to Frederick was to bring Fern over to meet Grandma Carrie. What a powerful medicine that was for Carrie's outlook on life. Carrie was thrilled to be a grandmother!

Around the middle of October, a wound developed on Carrie's abdomen next to the ostomy. I sent a picture to Dr. Pierre, who wanted to see Carrie as soon as possible. Dr. Pierre was sufficiently concerned that the proximity of the wound to the ostomy would make wound healing impossible. Available options were limited—wait for healing while risking infection or reverse the ostomy. The rationale for the reversal was simple—schedule the procedure for mid-January at a point when, theoretically, any remnants of immune-mediated colitis would have resolved.

Fortunately, during this period, I procured a wheelchair accessible van and was able to take Carrie to visit her mom at the retirement center. It was great to get the two of them together after nearly a five-month hiatus. Back in late 2020, during the initial COVID lockdowns, Margaret's cognitive abilities had deteriorated significantly due to the social isolation, even with Zoom calls. When in-person visits returned in 2021, Margaret was initially confused but warmed up quickly after her mind processed Carrie's smiling face. Similarly, in 2022, after nearly five months of not seeing Carrie, Margaret was fuzzy, but she soon recognized the 10,000-watt smile. It was good medicine for both mother and daughter, even though they were now sitting next to each other in matching wheelchairs.

During those months after Carrie's hospital discharge, we had many visitors. Several people dropped off meals, and many others sent cards and letters. One sign of Carrie's hastening decline that I should have recognized was her lack of interest in reading. She had been a voracious reader, but after the fall on June 8th, she lost her zeal for the written word. I should have done a better job of picking up on that cue. Perhaps I should have started pulling out the many picture albums and scrapbooks she had created over the years. At that point, where she still had some energy, I think she would have appreciated slowly turning those pages. Hindsight. Always 20/20.

CARRIE'S JOURNAL - APRIL 9, 1978

There are so many things I would have done differently—I guess hindsight is better than foresight.

With the help of our aide, I was able to get Carrie dressed and into her wheelchair to go to an early Christmas Eve service. Afterward, I pulled off a subdued Christmas Eve dinner. Carrie got her wheelchair up to the table to join me, Danny, Ben, and Renee. It was a far cry from what I prepared the previous year, but Carrie didn't complain. She was happy enough that I was able to get her out of bed with the Hoyer lift, put her in the wheelchair, and have her sit at the table. I'm not sure if she ate more than a spoonful, but she was thankful for the opportunity to take part in her favorite annual tradition. The boys dutifully took turns reading through the verses in our Advent calendar. Carrie was adamant that Fern, even though an infant, would be present to witness this event so that the tradition would continue with the next generation.

By early January, anxiety about the pending surgery had consumed Carrie. Her constant question was, "What if the colitis returns?", to which the surgeon, the oncologist, and I all replied that it was highly unlikely.

Surgery was scheduled for Tuesday, January 17th, and we dutifully showed up early at the hospital. Our home health aide helped Carrie get ready and went with us through the admission process before saying goodbye as I wheeled Carrie into the pre-op area. Carrie was highly anxious, and I held her hand and stayed by her side throughout pre-op. I just hoped that my presence would reassure her that things would work out. I was optimistic that the colitis would not return. I was less certain about how we would manage Carrie's bowel functions after the procedure, given that she would require transferring to a portable commode whenever she needed to have a bowel movement.

The procedure took several hours, and I joined Carrie and sat at her side in the recovery area while she slept off the residual effects from anesthesia. Back in her room, she was mostly comfortable, but the wound created by the reversal now made the previous wound that existed next to the ostomy look like a minor sore. A plan was put into place to apply a "wound vacuum" to speed the recovery process. Carrie managed to progress for the first two days, but by Thursday afternoon, the first hints of colitis made themselves known. At first, the surgeon was not overly concerned as she thought the bowel was only slowly waking up after being dormant for nearly six months. But by the weekend, full-blown damage control was underway as nothing would stop the bowels from spontaneously evacuating.

Carrie's worst nightmare had become reality.

She didn't cry or decompensate, but looking back, it seems likely that at that point, Carrie started to give up. She just seemed to accept that this was just another bad thing happening to her.

To her credit, she never threw it back in my face that I previously told her it was unlikely that the colitis would return. Doesn't matter. I remain bothered by naively thinking that this terrible outcome would never come to fruition.

After a few failed medical interventions, Carrie asked Dr. Pierre to go back in and "reverse the reversal," and a permanent ostomy procedure was performed on January 23rd. As with the surgery in August, Carrie was far from ready for discharge as her overall condition had deteriorated to what is referred to in health care as a "train wreck." Her nutritional status and electrolytes were severely compromised, resulting in wild swings of cardiac arrhythmias, a disturbing finding of deep-vein thrombosis, and increasing anxiety, especially in the evenings. There were fewer distractions from the medical and nursing staff in the evening, and as Carrie frequently napped during the day, her mind would wander in those evening hours, perseverating over all the things that could go wrong. Getting the medical issues resolved extended the hospitalization out to the middle of February. The anxiety would continue until she went into her final sleep.

Upon discharge, I decided that I needed to sleep on the sofa next to her bed to be more readily available to help if things came up during the night (and they did). Frederick Health showed up in force the next day with various teams: palliative care, wound care, PT, OT, and the home health aide. With the palliative care nurse, Carrie made a significant change to her Order for Life Sustaining Treatment form—and waived most of the available treatments. She did not waive all, but it was a big indication that she did not want to return to the hospital. Shortly after discharge, Carrie demonstrated signs and symptoms of severe dehydration, and the Frederick Health nurse was able to coordinate with the home IV company to get intravenous fluids added to her daily regimen. Carrie's nutritional situation remained bleak as she had lost a good portion of her appetite and rarely consumed more than 500 calories per day despite my encouraging her to eat more. I reverted to adding ice cream to Ensure in a blender, which Carrie found appealing, but she was rarely able to consume a full serving.

Carrie left it up to me to work with Dr. Mansky on the next step in her cancer treatment. She had not yet totally given up hope, but her lack of engagement in the process should have sent up big flashing lights to me that I was too consumed in keeping her alive to notice. Carrie had been off treatment altogether since her bathroom fall in early June of 2022. Dr. Mansky identified a new treatment based on the genetic characteristics of her cancer. Carrie started the oral treatment on February 20th. As part of the order for the new treatment, blood samples for lab tests were drawn shortly after the initiation of therapy. Those results came back on March 2nd.

The results were not good.

It was unlikely that the new therapy caused the terrible metabolic state that Carrie experienced. Her dietary intake, even with intravenous hydration, was not sufficient to maintain normal blood chemistry levels. What was more disturbing to me was the precipitous drop in her white blood cell count. Given that she had a new ostomy and an ugly wound from where the old ostomy was located, the drop in white count could be an invitation to a fulminating infection.

Dr. Mansky called to discuss correcting her electrolytes and recommended that Carrie consider returning to the hospital.

When I talked with Carrie about Dr. Mansky's recommendation, she told me that she thought it was time to call hospice.

I was surprised, but I also wasn't.

I was ready to keep on doing whatever it took to keep Carrie going, but I also perceived that she had lost interest in fighting. Her food intake was abysmal. Her fatigue was nearly constant. And her willingness to see visitors had fallen to a new low. All of the signs were there—if I had taken a moment to step back and observe.

I nodded my head and told her I understood. What else could I do?

A brave decision on Carrie's part and something I knew in my head was always a possibility. In my heart, I held out hope that Carrie, as a member of a family that had generations of octogenarians and older, would always outlive me, but in my head, I knew better. I had explored many papers from the oncology literature, and none were encouraging. And Carrie, what did she know? Carrie didn't spend too much time trying to find answers to how this last encounter with cancer would play out, as she knew in her heart for several months that her days were numbered.

We waited through the weekend to make the call to hospice so that the intake interview could take place when both Dan and Ben could take part in the conversation and ask any questions.

Throughout this long weekend, my head was in a thousand different places. Things were happening so fast that I wasn't able to process what was right in front of me. There were so many things

I wanted to do—but where to begin? My focus turned to what I could do, and that was to make Carrie as comfortable as possible.

The hospice social worker showed up on Tuesday afternoon, March 7th, for the enrollment process. The hospice nurses arrived on Wednesday, the 8th, and went through instructions concerning the various medicines they would provide: lorazepam, haloperidol, and hydromorphone—all in liquid form for easy administration and absorption.

It was time for Carrie to go about the business of actively dying.

Carrie entered hospice twelve days prior to her death, and with everything else that Carrie did in her life, she excelled at dying. She sped through all the hospice timeline benchmarks for death and made the suggested ranges look like mere traffic suggestions. Up until two weeks prior, she made a valiant effort to stay alive, but the cancer and the accumulation of complications from the many treatments she had undergone over nearly fifteen years caught up with her. She was now far beyond a tipping point—she was in free fall. There were very few tears when she decided to enter hospice care. The most that Carrie cried about was the thought of leaving our recently born granddaughter, Fern. Carrie wanted so much to be involved in her life. She did not regret that she would leave to me the important task of making sure that Fern grew up to know everything about Grandma Carrie—she just wanted to be a part of that experience.

Me, I was just numb. I was experiencing whiplash from my converse roles of doing everything possible to keep her alive into someone now helping her to make the final transition.

The hospice staff were wonderful in preparing our family for Carrie's passing and making it as peaceful as possible, but they could not prepare me for every contingency. On the first day, they showed up with their stash of medicines intended to keep Carrie comfortable on her journey. I asked what I was to do regarding her regular maintenance medicines—the medicines to prevent atrial fibrillation and control her blood pressure. Up until that point, I had meticulously tracked every dosage taken and every change in her medications. When our world is turned upside down, our minds tend to focus on those few things that we know we can control. The nurse gave me a strange look as if to suggest that I might be missing the point of hospice. It took me a moment, but I finally understood and slowly nodded to signal my understanding.

On day four in hospice (Saturday night and early Sunday, March 11th and 12th), Carrie thrashed about, unable to get comfortable. I was up all night moving pillows and trying to figure out the optimal dose of lorazepam and hydromorphone to help her sleep. Lorazepam, also known by the trade name Ativan, is for anxiety, and the hydromorphone is for pain, with the trade name Dilaudid. The dosages prescribed by hospice were not working, and although it had been nearly thirty years since I had last regularly worked as a pharmacist, I thought I could find that sweet spot that would get her more comfortable.

At about 3:30 in the morning, when another request came in to rearrange pillows, I shouted, "Carrie, for the love of God, I need to get some sleep if I am going to take care of you!"

Everything became eerily quiet, and Carrie reverted almost to a childlike state. She finally replied, "OK, I'm going to do better."

And she did. No Ague smart talk back, just a realization that I was at wits' end and that, even though she knew she was going to die soon, she could not get twenty-four hours a day out of me without it adversely affecting the care I provided.

We both got a few hours of sleep, and on Sunday morning, I talked with Sissy about my experience. I felt terrible for the way I had reacted the night before. Carrie, to her credit, never asked why I yelled at her. She probably forgot about the incident as she was in somewhat of a fever dream throughout that night, but I will carry to my grave the shame of acting like a horse's ass because of a few hours of lost sleep. It's difficult to know how that night would have ended if I hadn't blown up at her, but I am sure I would have felt better about myself in the morning.

Sissy asked why I didn't call hospice in the middle of the night. I wasn't sure. I guess I didn't want to bother anyone. When I did talk with hospice, they assured me they have a twenty-four-hour service, and a nurse was at the house later that morning to reassess Carrie's medication needs. A resolution was quickly found in the form of fentanyl patches, with an adjunct of morphine syrup and an increased lorazepam dosage. We did not experience any similar situations the remainder of Carrie's following week on this earth.

Sissy arrived later that day, and my sister-in-law Karen arrived on Monday. Both would help me for the remainder of the week. Cousins Barb and Mary Ellen visited from Ohio on Wednesday, March 15th, and it lifted Carrie's spirits to be able to say goodbye to them. Diane, the pathologist and former nurse, arrived later Wednesday afternoon. Several members of our neighborhood and church, as well as Carrie's teaching friends, stopped in to say goodbye. It was too difficult of a process for others—and that is something I can respect.

Carrie ended up sleeping a good deal of the time but had a few hours of lucidity through Thursday of the week. In one of the more coherent periods, she explained to me her thoughts on what I should do with our house after she was gone. I had long before determined that I could not stay in the home filled with so many improvements Carrie had orchestrated. By opening the door on the topic, Carrie relieved me of any guilt I would have in the process.

It was in the middle of an afternoon early in the week. Karen and Sissy were in the kitchen sorting through our cupboards, partly to give Carrie and me some privacy, and partly because Karen is the kind of person who cannot sit still. Karen thought she could help me get a head start on organizing my life as a widower. Sissy was there to make sure Karen didn't go too far, as Sissy understood that after living in that house for twenty-seven years, I understood Carrie's organizational layout. They were both right in their respective ways. And at that time, what they were doing was the last thing on my mind. Carrie was oblivious to all the goings on, but she knew that I was there only for her.

Out of nowhere, she said, "You don't want to stay in this house, do you?"

I answered honestly. "This place would be too much for me to manage. And do I really need all of these empty rooms? I think it might be easier if I moved on to something smaller."

Carrie was satisfied with my short answer. I held back in admitting that the primary reason was the thought of living in our home without her. As I surveyed the house, I saw nothing but her fingerprints on the improvements. While I didn't foresee the house haunting me with her memory, I knew I needed a different environment in which to learn to move forward. I tucked away the discussion in my mental to-do list for after Carrie was gone.

On another occasion, Carrie woke up and out of nowhere asked me to kiss her, which I did, gently, before turning away quickly so that she would not see my tears.

We often simply stated that we loved each other and had always loved only each other. A big regret I have is that, given Carrie's condition with an ileostomy, a left leg nearly paralyzed due to a radiation injury, and a left shoulder fracture not completely healed, it was impossible for me to just hold her in my arms. I would have loved to have had that opportunity to just hold her for a few moments. I think Carrie would have liked it too.

One of the more difficult conversations with Carrie involved a discussion about funerals with Linda Warehime, our church visitation pastor. Yes, plural. Carrie was concerned about the plans for her ninety-six-year-old mother, Margaret. While Carrie understood that I would be more than capable of handling those tasks, as the only child, she felt this was another responsibility she did not want to put on my shoulders. But it had to be done. During our discussion with Linda, it was obvious that Carrie wished she could explain things better. She frequently mixed up items that she wanted for her service with those she wanted for Margaret. It was heartbreaking as Linda and I repeated back what we thought we'd heard. Carrie was frustrated that we were confusing her intentions. After some aggravation for all three of us, we finally got it straight. Carrie smiled.

On Friday, March 17th, Carrie became mostly unresponsive. I thought for sure she would die that day. She didn't, and at one point woke up and said the simple word, "Why?"

Sissy was with me, and we looked at each other in confusion. Upon reflection, we concluded that Carrie was asking why she was not yet dead, not why this was happening to her.

The same state of non-responsiveness continued into Saturday, the 18th.

When Carrie died on Sunday morning, it was a peaceful passing. Karen had been keeping vigil with me since 4 a.m., and we knew the end was near. Karen had been through this with a brother, a sister, and both her father and mine. She knew the signs. Diane, who had been catnapping, joined us just prior to Carrie's passing. We sat for a few minutes, allowing Carrie's spirit to pass before we did anything. It was a moment of so many emotions for the three of us sitting around that bed, yet we couldn't adequately express any of what we were feeling. Carrie was gone and yet she looked so present and peaceful. So, we sat there and appreciated the short time as if moving would somehow disturb her final rest.

Before long, we looked at each other, and I simply stated, "Time to make the notifications."

I thought back on how fast our twenty-seven years in Frederick had flown by, in the blink of an eye, taking us to this moment. Yet, some of the memories were also etched in my mind as if recorded in super slow motion. And what had I learned from Carrie to help me move forward?

Taking the Unknown Step Forward (1997–2002)

We departed McDonald on the morning of August 1, 1997, for the real estate closing appointment in Frederick scheduled at 4 p.m. Our moving truck would not arrive until the next day, and the former owners were kind enough to allow us to get started on a few things in the house before closing. We arranged to have a carpet cleaner show up early that afternoon, a serendipitous scheduling. As with other moves, Margaret was there to help. She kept the kids entertained while Carrie and I started to clean up a few things around the house. Carrie decided to pull the refrigerator out to clean the floor behind the appliance. What Carrie did not know was that there was a copper tube that ran from the floor into the refrigerator for the ice maker. Carrie did not appreciate her own strength and the tube broke free from the refrigerator causing a small flood. A minor meltdown was in the making. There was no screaming or shouting. She clenched her fists and rolled up her shoulders as if she was ready to shout. Perhaps she would have been better off to just let it all out. Who knows? Having recognized the start of the symptomology, I jumped into damage control mode.

"Carrie, this is not a problem. I'll find the shut-off valve."

Getting the spill cleaned up was not problematic, but Carrie continued to stew. We departed for the closing all the while with Carrie mumbling that this wasn't the right house. She would later apologize—in her own sort of way.

I departed for Ohio a few days after the move-in to defend my dissertation while Carrie got busy putting together her application in the FCPS. She was certain that she would not be able to get hired this late into the summer. Much to Carrie's surprise, the personnel office set her up with three interviews the next day. She took a language arts teaching job that was a 0.6 position at a middle school not far from our house, but not in the same catchment area as where the boys would attend. This was a great schedule as I could get the boys off to school before leaving for work, and Carrie would be home before they got off the bus.

Carrie announced her hiring by coming home with a thirty-six-inch television for the finished basement—a sort of peace offering for her meltdowns over the past few months. Back in 1997, that size television qualified as a big screen, as the flat screens had yet to make their way to the market. And those thirty-six-inch televisions were heavy. Any concerns about the home loan were quickly forgotten.

Finding a church was another task high on Carrie's list, and though we had not been in the area for two weeks, she identified two churches known to have good youth programs. The first church, Brook Hill United Methodist, was the closer of the two. We never made it to the second church as we found a vibrant congregation at Brook Hill, which continued through Carrie's celebration of life ceremony conducted there twenty-seven years later.

The next activity was to help the kids adjust to the new neighborhood, and what better way than with a dog? We visited the nearby county animal shelter and picked out a female puppy that we named "Sam," short for Samantha. Sam was an energetic full-bred mutt—part beagle, part husky, and probably parts of a dozen other breeds. Most importantly, the dog was remarkably good-natured.

As the school year started, Carrie and the boys got into their daily routines. The kids were making friends, especially Danny, and Ben usually hung out with Danny's friends.

Life was good. Usually. At one point in that fall of 1997, sitting around the dinner table, we boys were unaware that Carrie had a bad day. We probably were not picking up on any signals and were likely inconsiderate of the meal Carrie had prepared, despite her bad day. We bantered on as if the world revolved around our activities. Carrie, meanwhile, slowly withdrew into herself, and we didn't notice until it was too late. This one was serious. There was no shouting or screaming, just this look of extreme emotional distress. The boys and I looked at each other—What was going on? Carrie stormed out of the house, and I worried about her state of mind. We had no idea where she'd gone, but she called within a few hours to tell me that she got a hotel room for the night. She returned in the morning as if nothing had happened, and that was the last of her major meltdowns. She would, in the future, have minor episodes where she would get overly upset about things the boys would do.

These events were not necessarily depression-related, and if she were to have spoken with someone with more expertise in mental health, I would think they would have characterized them as anxiety attacks. Given that Owen would develop excessive anxiety in the last decade of his life, especially over the prospect of Carrie's cancer, you could say that Carrie had the Ague family tendency. And while anxiety is not a cause for cancer, it is well known to have an impact on the immune system functioning that keeps cancer from spreading. During the duration of Carrie's treatment, I often thought back on things in our lives that might have contributed to her cancer and frequently came back to the way in which she dealt with stress. Hindsight. A burden that I need to let go of.

Carrie would continue to make many connections among the faculty at Ballenger Creek, with many of these leading to lifelong friendships. She also learned the ins and outs of the FCPS and decided on a career development goal where she knew she could make an even greater impact than in the classroom—a master's degree in school counseling. She began that journey in the winter term of 1998 with Western Maryland College, later renamed McDaniel College. Carrie pursued the course load through a gradual process as she found taking one course per term, along with teaching and parenting, was the right balance in her life. She eventually finished in May 2002.

The late fall of 1997 and winter of 1998 found us busy shuttling Danny to basketball practices and games after he made the Monocacy Middle basketball team in a league that was loosely affiliated with the school system. As the school year rolled along, the kids developed more friends within the neighborhood, and both Carrie and I developed friendships with those respective parents, associations that would be lifelong and that begat further friendships. They were also an entrance way to book clubs for both of us—a ladies' group for Carrie and a guys' club for me, although the guys' group was not as serious about the books. After our first drink, we solved many of the world's problems if anyone would have taken the time to listen to us. The escape into the book club was a form of therapy for me when Carrie was going through her last few years—not the books, especially, but the camaraderie of the group. Did I mention that three of the members were clinical psychologists? In those later years when Carrie was sick, one of the spouses from the group would come over and sit with Carrie while I was away for those few hours.

The school years of 1998 through 2002 found Carrie teaching full-time at Ballenger Creek Middle School and getting more involved with friends at that location. Ben joined Danny at Monocacy Middle School in 1998. Ben blended in with Danny's friends as the somewhat nerdy but lovable and brainy brother. Life continued to be a bit congested with Carrie's master's program and the kids' activities. Owen and Margaret were frequent visitors, and they would also bring Sissy's mom, Anna Mae, as a passenger on every trip. It was always great fun getting the entire group together at Sissy's for Christmas dinner. Carrie would continue with her annual show trips to NYC with Sissy, but the moms gave up the activity about the time they hit the latter part of their seventh decade.

The boys continued through middle school and into high school without too many incidents. They both appreciated the opportunity to make new friends and take part in multiple sports. And as with most kids during this period, they weathered the storm and aftermath of 9/11. Carrie continued to make lasting friendships at Ballenger Creek Middle, along with neighborhood and church friends.

By the end of the fall of 2002, we knew I would be heading to Korea in May 2003. My pending promotion to colonel included an obligation of three additional years in the Army if I wanted to retire at that rank. Carrie thought it appropriate to accept the promotion, but was not excited about a pending move. By taking what is known as an "unaccompanied" tour for one year to Korea, as opposed to moving with my family for an "accompanied" tour of two years, we were guaranteed an additional year of stability in Frederick. While there was no certainty beyond that year, it was likely that I would be assigned somewhere in the DC region upon return. We— and by the use of the term "we," I probably meant "I"—had rationalized that the kids would be old enough when I went on this unaccompanied tour to be a help at home with their mom. A pipedream on my part. Carrie knew from the early outset after we married that a typical military career usually involved one overseas "long tour" with your family and one "short unaccompanied tour." The long tour to Germany was fabulous. But neither of us looked forward to the short tour. We also didn't know what would be the best time for a short tour, as the phrase "best time" should probably read as "least bad time." As such, we started to prepare ourselves mentally for the challenge.

Carrie finished the classes for her master's degree in the fall, and I helped her with the research paper for her master's project by creating tables and sorting the data. Regardless of Carrie's experience at the computer camp in the '70s, she failed to find interest in the many functions available in Excel or similar programs. The research topic, for which she had some passion, was the effect of frequent moves on middle-school-age kids. To the casual observer, it would appear this was due to her experience as a military spouse who saw the applicability in that setting. And that's what I initially thought. Carrie used small words to educate me on the topic. I guess I was a bit of a brick when it came to the issues faced in school. Carrie explained that the military kids typically had structured upbringings. The real target of her research was the group of kids who moved because of issues associated with homelessness, a topic I was blissfully ignorant about, but one that Carrie would later encounter on a regular basis as a middle school counselor.

As the time for my departure to Korea drew close, Carrie's anxiety gradually increased. Even though we knew we would have far greater opportunities for communication than my deployment to Desert Storm, and that my personal safety was not in question, Carrie could barely look at me on the morning of my departure as she was overwhelmed about the coming year. This was not a harbinger of good tidings for the coming year of separation.

FEBRUARY 27, 1977

I'm terribly depressed. I don't know why.

CHAPTER 8

A Life After a Life

Love each day to the fullest
Get the most from each hour
Each day and each age of your life
Then you can look forward with confidence and back without regret

– Edgar A. Guest

Carrie Ann (Ague) Pierson went home at 7 a.m. on a quiet Sunday morning, March 19, 2023. Officially, her death certificate reads she died of endometrial cancer. But Carrie died *with* endometrial cancer, as her demise was far more complicated.

After Diane, Karen, and I ended our time of silent prayer and reflection, I notified Dan and Ben, followed by hospice, Sissy, and Linda Warehime. Diane and Karen took care of crafting a text to my siblings. I texted the boys to come to the house to see their mom before the funeral home arrived. Texted the boys, you ask? It was a generational thing. Even at thirty-seven and thirty-five years old, they rarely answered their phones. When all were congregated, we gathered in a group hug. There was little talking as there was nothing really to say. I knew they, like me, regretted that we could not prevent the events Carrie endured over the last few years.

Sissy had gone home the previous night to get some much-needed rest as she had kept vigil for at least three nights that week. Now she, along with husband Mike, returned. Linda Warehime had always been close with Carrie and arrived to help us prepare to send Carrie's body off.

The hospice nurse was just wonderful getting Carrie cleaned up and ready to go, even though her remains would be cremated. Her ashes will eventually be interned with mine at Arlington National Cemetery. Sissy and Karen helped me find an appropriate dress for Carrie to wear on that last earthly trip, knowing that Carrie always liked to travel in style. Upstairs in the guest bedroom was a suit that her mom had already set aside to be buried in. Margaret said she didn't want to be cold going six feet under. Carrie, though, having made her wish for cremation known, had made no prior clothing selection. Karen and Sissy quickly sorted through the many available choices and recommended a long shift with a bold pattern—one they agreed had always looked good on Carrie.

I was sold. Carrie would leave this world dressed as if she were ready to take it over.

The funeral home staff was beyond exceptional. What a pro we had with us. He knew all the right things to say and encouraged us every step of the way. After the hearse pulled into the driveway, he met us in the garage before entering the house and gathered the boys and me together for a sort of perspective setting.

"You know that body we are going to take out of here in a few minutes is not Carrie. Carrie is not with us anymore. Carrie is with the angels."

That simple introduction made it so much easier to allow her body to be carted away.

After the hearse departed, I said to the boys, "We should let grandma know."

Ever since Margaret's stroke in late 2017, no one was really sure what she comprehended. But when we crossed the threshold of her room at the retirement center, Margaret knew why we were there to see her. And on that otherwise bright Sunday morning, Margaret understood. Her eyes told us.

I didn't spend long with Margaret, as I had an aching need to return to the house and transform it from a hospice setting back to the realm of the living. I don't know what crawled up inside me to feel like this had to be done right away. Maybe just sitting around awaiting death for the last eleven days had made me want to do something to rid the house of what I perceived as a sickly air. The room was returned to normal within a few hours. I knew that visitors would be showing up soon to help me through the day, and I was not disappointed in that regard. Having our friends stop by was more than comforting.

After visitors departed that day, it was time to move into full preparation mode—not for a funeral, but for a celebration of life—for Carrie had led a life worth celebrating. Fortunately, Pastor Dana, the lead pastor at our church, had previously identified potential dates, and Carrie, being who she was, departed this earth in a time that would make the first option work for all involved. The service was scheduled for Thursday, the 23rd. It was a busy time, and I was engaged nonstop until everyone left.

In addition to my siblings and their respective spouses, Carrie's childhood friend Laurie and her husband Don agreed to come and take part in the service. Laurie and Don are both accomplished vocalists. Don had recently retired from a tax consulting firm and was now getting ready for his calling as an associate pastor at the church where Carrie and I were married in 1980. Deb Jefferson and Cathy Kazio returned again from their respective homes in North Carolina and Florida. The out-of-towners, as well as some of our neighbors, converged on our house the night before the service for a relaxing spread of various foods. But as I am writing, over two years removed from that day, I cannot remember what we ate or where the food came from, and I am not sure if I ate anything. Sissy and Karen co-chaired the effort to bring everything together, and I, per my usual modus operandi, just showed up. Carrie would have recognized that pattern, but given what I was going through, she was up in heaven cutting me some slack.

Linda Warehime knew that I was in zombie mode and completed the itinerary for the service, as she had been at our home when Carrie had expressed her desires. Don and Laurie contacted me earlier that week about the selections for the songs, and I muddled my way through their recommendations and found two that we all agreed were appropriate. The night before, I outlined the content of what I thought would be a relatively short discussion of my life with Carrie. From my few talking points, the memory would go on to last the better part of an hour. Perhaps I could have left out some of the off-the-cuff tangents and rabbit holes that I went down. Strangely enough, the congregation appreciated learning about Carrie's life, and I hope that Carrie was looking down with approval. I closed with a request for the congregation to sing a song for Fern that Carrie requested: "Jesus Loves Me."

Deb Jefferson and Cathy Kazio followed with their memories of Carrie as a friend and counselor. What a blessing it was to have them return from their respective out-of-state homes to honor Carrie. They shared powerful stories of Carrie's gifts as a counselor and a friend. Linda provided an appropriate sermon for Carrie, words that helped the boys and me in our transition to life without Carrie. Danny chose the closing song, "Seasons of Love," from the

Broadway musical *Rent,* as he knew it was one of Carrie's favorites.

We returned to the house on this relatively warm early spring day, and visitors just streamed in and out onto the porch and mingled about everywhere. In addition to Cathy and Deb making long trips, relatives and friends from Eugene, Oregon; Reno, Nevada; Chicago; and Detroit arrived to say farewell to Carrie. Various friends who were on the faculty or staff at Ballenger Creek Middle School and Crestwood Middle School showed up, as well as friends who went on the annual trip to Broadway, church friends, neighborhood and Army friends, and several colleagues from the NIH. It was all very special.

Yet I cannot recall a single conversation, only being appreciative that they showed up to honor Carrie. It was heartwarming to see them all, regardless of my trance-like state. It was still too much to process, so I didn't bother to try. Again, food that day showed up as if it were the Biblical five loaves and two fish. I had no idea where it came from, but I think it was a lot of leftovers from the night before and from the lunch at the church. Others stepped up and took care of getting things out, and I showed up—and again, probably did not eat.

As the crowd in the house started to dwindle, Dan, Ben, and my siblings remained to keep me company—what a great family. Eventually, everyone departed.

I sat alone in the house and reflected on where I was in life. I had just said goodbye to my life partner of forty-three years. All I could see was a collage of life events swirling through my subconsciousness. These were all good memories: the 1974 football game with the awkward teenage girl, the trips down to Oxford when I could not wait to see Carrie, going shopping to find furniture for that tiny little house at Fort Leavenworth, the many trips around the country and across the world, and, of course, the arrival of both of our sons. But what stood out was our 2019 dinner along the Tagus River in Lisbon, where we just sat as if time stood still.

After going to bed that night, I fell fast asleep. Exhaustion won out over my spinning brain. The conflicting states would later reverse themselves.

I had no concept at that time of the range of emotions that would hit me over the next several months.

FEBRUARY 8, 1977

Life was sort of slow and easy.

JANUARY 31, 1977

Life is moving so fast. I've got to do all I can in the small amount of time I have, so I can leave my small, insignificant mark on the world of which I'm a part.

Being Apart 2002–2003 (Jerry in Korea)

Telephone communications were kept to once a week, primarily because of the twelve-hour time difference, and were conducted over the landline. We filled in the blanks with daily emails. I don't recall anything alarming in our messaging, even when chaotic things were going on. Email was not the best way to communicate the complexities of life.

Before that summer, our house had become somewhat of a hangout for Danny's friends, and Carrie encouraged it as she wanted to know what the kids were up to rather than Danny heading to points unknown. But during that summer, the hanging out became somewhat more routine until after the group graduated from high school. While at times the kids could be downright obnoxious, to thank Carrie for "volunteering" our home, several of the kids from Danny's class were later included in the senior yearbook listing of extracurricular activities: "Pierson Basement, freshman through senior year."

Carrie and the boys flew to Korea for ten days in late July and early August. I booked us a suite at the Dragon Hill Lodge, the Army's guest house in Seoul, as my bachelor officer quarters were not adequate for family living. Considering the long direct flight time, over twelve hours, they were "toast" by the time they landed. We barely finished dinner and got up to the suite before they all collapsed and fell asleep.

We had a great time as a family, with visits to many of the city's cultural sites, outdoor markets, and dining opportunities with Korean colleagues from the hospital. We received many invitations for dinner at various restaurants, and our hosts were always impressed with how well the boys had adjusted their palates to Korean food.

The 2002–2003 school year started with a new routine for everyone. Danny now had a driver's license, so there was no longer the issue of waiting on the bus. Carrie smartly made the decision to limit herself to a half-time teaching position as she knew she needed to be more available for the boys in my absence. Sometimes that availability clashed with expectations Danny had, and while both the kids had, at various points in their lives, displayed an attitude, this would become a persistent issue between Danny and Carrie throughout the year. And while we encouraged their friends to hang out in the basement, having a basement full of teenagers with attitude sometimes became unbearable for Carrie.

Fortunately, I scheduled leave for mid-October, a bit early in the cycle of the year, but the timing would prove fortuitous. In the twelve days of leave, I was able to watch a few of the kids' football games and did my best to understand the brewing rift between Carrie and Danny. The problem was not always at the surface, and Danny tamped down on the outward expressions while I was at home.

Before long, I was on the nonstop flight from Dulles back to Seoul. Fortunately, and the use of that word sounds somewhat insane given the situation, I would get called back from Korea to Fort Detrick for a short-term project just before Christmas. The ripple effects of 9/11 were now having an impact on our family. The initial military response in 2001 in Afghanistan was somewhat limited and did not result in the mobilization of many medical units. As the fall of 2002 progressed, the Bush administration continued to make claims that Iraq was harboring weapons of mass destruction and threatened military action. As one of those weapons of concern was nerve agents, my somewhat unique skill in regulatory work was a sought-after commodity. The two-star general at Fort Detrick made an entreaty to my boss in Korea about loaning me back for the purpose of helping put together the New Drug Application for the use of pyridostigmine bromide for nerve agent pretreatment. It meant that I was coming home for the duration of this project, and we did not know how long it would take to finish.

I arrived at Dulles on December 23rd. Carrie knew I was returning but did not tell the boys; she correctly determined it would make for a nice surprise and a much merrier Christmas for everyone. I stayed through the end of January on the project, but it was not like I was on leave. Each day, I was consumed with work activities. Unlike our time in October when Carrie returned from school long before the boys got home, we had no leisure time to ourselves during this visit. We returned to a few regular routines:

dinner with the boys, a few social functions with friends, and attending church together.

My departure this time was not traumatic, as we were looking at three months remaining on the Korean assignment. I was on orders back to Fort Detrick to return to my former job. Things were looking up.

The direction of that good feeling would soon change. The US invasion of Iraq resulted in the mobilization of a substantial number of medical units, and one of those units included the guy who was to replace me in Korea. By the end of March, major military operations in Iraq were over, but the return of units was another matter. As the conflict evolved from a force on force to an insurgency, the need for medical personnel would not diminish. In early April, I found that my replacement was delayed in Iraq and that my assignment in Korea would be extended.

Carrie was going through a series of mini crises at the time. On her way home from work one day, a car driven by a person who had just held up a local fast-food restaurant crashed into her vehicle. Carrie was not injured, and the driver of the other car sped away and was never caught. Additionally, Danny had recently broken a bone in his hand in a locker-room fight after lacrosse practice—a strange story that ended up being about him protecting someone else. Carrie was at wits' end, and my news on the extended stay in Korea didn't help matters. Years later, Carrie would look back on this time as relatively trivial compared to the sacrifices made by other families whose lives were continually being disrupted with repeat deployments. She eventually considered her circumstances lucky in that we were spared those problems.

When I explained to my boss that Carrie had experienced some minor setbacks, he was more than happy to grant me leave to go home and smooth things over. As school was letting out for the summer, I was on a plane back to the States. Carrie was still a bit frazzled but readily recovered to make a few plans. She thought it a good idea for me to take the boys on an excursion to visit state universities in Ohio. This would give me time with the boys and her time to herself. After our excursion, I was soon on my way back to Seoul, and this time we had an end in sight. I returned to Maryland in early August, and we put the year of separation in the rear-view mirror.

Those were fifteen of the longest months of our lives, but in retrospect, that year did fly by. However, during the remaining nineteen years of Carrie's life, I made it a point not to talk about the great experiences I had traveling the Korean Peninsula when Carrie was definitely not having a good time back in Maryland. And to Carrie's credit, she did not harp on me about the bad year she had endured. I appreciated that she moved forward in a positive way from that low point.

2003–2008

Our last stretch of cancer-free years was a transitional time for all of us. Danny started his last year in high school shortly after I returned from Korea. For Ben, it was a hyper-charged academic year and one in which he would make his first mark on the football field. The biggest change, though, was for Carrie, who spent the 2003–2004 year completing her practicums in counseling at Monocacy Middle School. She was no longer with her beloved group of friends from Ballenger Creek, but they would stay linked through monthly dinners, as several of them had also moved on to other schools. Even though Carrie had her master's in counseling, in order to work in the field, she needed certification from the State of Maryland, which required the practicum.

The boys had fun playing football even though the team that year was terrible. As bad as they were, Danny received an award from the local Baltimore Ravens fan club for his role on the team. Ben gained the notice of multiple Ivy League schools as the big kid with killer SAT scores.

For Carrie, the start of the 2004–2005 school year would bring another transition as she was assigned, along with Deb Boyce Jefferson, as the inaugural counseling team at the newly opening Crestwood Middle School. Carrie and Deb would grow into a dynamic team along with Cathy Kazio, who joined them the following year. These ladies remained close, lifelong friends. That first year, it was just Deb and Carrie, and there was much work to be done in getting the new school ready for its first year. Added to that confusion, I was starting a new job in the Army in a command position at the US Army Medical Materiel Development Activity. At the change of command ceremony, I did not hesitate to thank Carrie for her support in getting me to this point in my Army career.

The last thing we needed to do was get Danny out the door to OSU. Carrie took the lead on this trip and loaded up her vehicle to schlep Danny and his belongings to Columbus. As much of a pain as Danny had been to Carrie during the previous two years, when she returned to Maryland, she told me she had tears in her eyes when she departed Park Hall, the same dormitory where she had dropped me off in the fall of 1975. Ben, witnessing the discussion, could not understand why I gave her a big hug when she told me about it.

As the fall proceeded, Ben had an opportunity to make an on-campus visit to Yale for a football game. Owen and Margaret were more than happy to drive him up to New Haven. During the winter, Carrie continued on her NYC show trip weekend while I took Ben to Carnegie Mellon to meet with the football coach and cement his plans to attend CMU.

Before long, it was time to drop Ben off at school for football camp—where he lasted about two weeks before deciding football at the college level was not fun. At CMU, Ben made the mistake of taking his AP credit and starting at the next level up in his computer science and calculus classes. He had never studied much in high school and was not prepared for the intensity at which many of the students worked. Ben survived that first year at CMU but did not thrive.

Carrie's second year at Crestwood was less hectic than the first, especially when Cathy Kazio joined as a third counselor. In the spring of 2006, Carrie and I took a spring break trip by ourselves as we no longer had the kids' schedules weighing us down. The concept of a family summer vacation grew increasingly difficult to plan given the four different schedules. We flew to Charleston, South Carolina, in 2006 and had a great time touring and dining, thanks in large part to Carrie's planning. During that summer, Carrie and I traveled with friends Jerry and Paulette to visit Erica and Sov on Grand Island, New York, just outside Buffalo. The New Yorkers were former neighborhood friends who had relocated for Sov's work. This was the trip, as I mentioned previously, when Carrie had her first significant indication that something with her health was not right.

The 2006–2007 school year began with both boys returning to their respective schools. Carrie had banked a number of personal days in the nine years since she started with FCPS and used several to take her mom, Margaret, to Hawaii for her eightieth birthday. Sissy went along and the three ladies had a great time. Margaret proved to be an energetic traveler.

Later that fall, I went to Athens, Georgia, to interview for a department chair position with the pharmacy school at the

University of Georgia. Carrie had no intention of moving anywhere but thought it a good idea for me to go through the interview process, as my time as USAMMDA commander would come to an end in the summer of 2007. I would either retire or take another position in the Army.

In late November 2006, Carrie found something in the employment section of the *Washington Post* that would change my life: an advertisement for a position at the NIH inside the National Institute of Allergy and Infectious Diseases (NIAID). Carrie knew my background and thought it would be a good fit. I applied, but did not have great expectations that I would ever hear back.

In the spring of 2007, I was surprised to be invited to NIAID and went through a relatively strange interview process. It turned out that the position had gone through multiple postings without finding the right candidate. On this posting, they found my qualifications to be a good fit for what they needed. I accepted the position and submitted my retirement application to the Army.

The school year of 2007–2008 now found both boys at Ohio State. Miraculously, Danny was on target to graduate at the end of 2008. Ben, upon transferring from CMU, set forth in the chemical engineering program, starting a new four-year process since he had never taken chemistry while at CMU.

It was early in 2008 that Carrie informed me that she wanted to go the ER because of abdominal discomfort. And so concluded twenty-eight years of marriage living without cancer.

Now, it was on to the unknown. In retrospect, I am thankful for each day of those twenty-eight years—and more importantly, the following fifteen years of living with Carrie through her cancer journey. I treasure the entirety of the forty-three years, the slow days and the fast days. For our relationship did last until the end for Carrie.

"One day, you're seventeen and you're planning for someday. And then quietly, without you ever really noticing, someday is today. And then someday is yesterday. And this is your life."

– John Green, Paper Towns

CHAPTER 9

The Aftermath

FEBRUARY 14, 1977

Will what we have last forever?

Eventually, everyone left and the house was empty, yet the loss didn't hit me immediately. The post-funeral activities had spared me from launching into grief. The death certificate soon arrived, and now it was time to make the necessary rounds. The business of dying is exhausting! I visited with banks, insurance people, social security, and the Maryland public school retirement system, as well as tried to crack the black box of changing my survivor benefit withhold in my military retirement. It seemed like every visit required additional visits. There was no time to grieve, and feeling numb throughout the process made it all that much more challenging to crack the code in this process.

And somehow, I managed with the help of a great real estate agent to do what Carrie recommended: find a new place to live and sell the old house. And of course, this busy work further postponed the eventual slide into grief, and that was a good thing.

At Easter though, I had my first indication that I was transitioning out of numbness and began sparring with grief. Our church, like many around the country, appropriately went to online services at the advent of the 2020 COVID outbreak. By the time regular attendance resumed, Carrie's health had deteriorated to the point that we continued with online services. We attended in person one time, on Christmas Eve in 2022. And of course, there was the celebration of life service a few weeks prior to Easter. Therefore, entering the sanctuary on Resurrection Sunday was probably not the best time for me to attempt a return to normal. I am not sure I comprehended what it meant to be normal at that time, and it was too soon to identify what the new normal would look like.

The happy message of resurrection was something I was not ready to receive on that bright spring morning. I was also not ready for small talk among the attendees who peppered me with questions on how I was doing. I felt strangely alone in this building full of smiling people. I quickly exited after the service and departed for home where I felt much less claustrophobic.

On the drive home, I realized that I had accepted Carrie's death as an appropriate ending of pain, but how was I to carry on without her? I am not sure what I was feeling, but it was quite different from anything I could have imagined. I spontaneously shed a tear whenever any songs came on the radio from the '70s era that dealt with the subject of loss from failed relationships. I felt I had failed Carrie in her last year of life. Falling asleep soon became a problem.

I also recognized that I wanted to record my feelings over time and had the first inkling I may want to write a book on experiencing loss. I found that the available literature tends to derive from the female perspective. Guys, let's face it. We really don't express our grief eloquently or openly. The subject of my literary journey would later change. The reason for my shift in writing focus was the discovery of Carrie's journal.

My sister-in-law Karen, as well as Sissy, returned during that week after Easter to help me go through Carrie's belongings. There were lots of clothes to go through as well as storage areas where various documents were stored. In one of those boxes of documents, Sissy came across a blue-bound journal—*The Journal*. Upon opening the journal, I immediately saw her first written words: *I got this last night. I decided that I'll write what I feel so I'll always have something to look back on to remember days past.*

Finding the journal would eventually cement my plans to continue this writing project. Also found was a large bin with several letters Carrie had received from students over the years. I later found that many letters were from her semester of student teaching that helped motivate her in the profession.

I didn't think too much about the journal at that time as we were busy going through so much stuff, and I was busy getting ready to move.

Throughout all of this activity, I visited Margaret several times a week. In the first few weeks, the news of Carrie's passing did not look like it had made an immediate, significant impact. She was eating less but did not yet look unhealthy. When Margaret first went into memory care late in 2017, Carrie visited a few times each week until COVID hit. With Carrie gone now, I was Margaret's primary family. Of course, the boys tried to see their grandmother as often as they could, and Sissy visited when possible, but I felt the burden of responsibility for Margaret.

Eventually, I was able to carve out some time to go through the journal. It was strange sitting in the empty house going through something as personal as that book, but the solitary space also made it seem like no one could look over my shoulder, and that the words Carrie wrote were shared only with me. There were entries that were not surprising since we had exchanged letters during this period. But there were also personal thoughts that caught me completely by surprise. A series of self-reflections, initiated by my reading of the journal, conspired to push me over the edge into grief. Falling asleep was difficult and only got worse. Also, I couldn't go through an hour without having a bout of the sniffles. I frequently felt resentment at our situation. Carrie's last nine months of illness and my loss of at least twenty more years of a continued tremendous relationship.

At about that time, I received an email from Kathleen, Carrie's friend, who recommended CrossFit when she saw my haggard appearance at the funeral. A new beginner's class was starting, and she gave me the details. I am not sure why I went, as I was still feeling substantially blue and was physically worn out from lack of sleep and the activities of getting the house ready to move. After completing the orientation classes, however, I decided to stay with the program, and while not a panacea for all that ailed, it was an endorphin booster. I owe much to the philosophy of Allison and Jason, the gym owners; Mollie, the general manager; and all the coaches who encouraged without coddling me to follow their philosophy of staying humble, happy, and healthy—although the happy part remained a bridge too far at that time. But just as important to me were the fellow gym participants who showed up every morning and not only accepted me but even now continue to provide encouragement.

I also had enough self-awareness to know that I needed professional medical intervention. I discussed what I was going through with my brother Ed, the psychiatrist. Of course, Ed could not consider me a patient, but he did recommend I talk with someone locally. As a first step, I sought help through my regular family practice clinic. An insightful young physician's assistant spent an hour discussing my situation, prescribed appropriate medication, and recommended the various support groups available through hospice. Those interventions, though not a cure all, were valuable.

Also sandwiched into this period were the activities of closing on my new and old homes and the physical move. And again, going through more boxes. I found in one of Margaret's boxes in our attic a stack of letters that Carrie wrote to her parents while in college—not all the letters, but many. I went about sorting the letters the best I could by academic year and date within the year. Most of the letters were about how classes were going, but I could hear Carrie's voice as she wrote, and I appreciated entries in which Carrie spoke about me.

I discovered another "gift" during the move as I emptied Carrie's nightstand. A small piece of paper with a note written on the back: "I hope this imagery helps." On the front was the poem "Gone from My Sight," which is attributed to a few authors. This version included the name of Henry Van Dyke. The words to the poem are at the opening of Part Two of this book.

Carrie wrote that note sometime before June 8, 2022, the day she fell and was never able to go back upstairs. I don't know exactly when she wrote that note, but whenever it was, she knew in her heart that she was not going to recover from the third bout with cancer. And I knew in my head that it was unlikely that she would recover, but my heart would not listen. I think Carrie also wanted me to find the note so that I would know she had figured things out, but how I wish we had talked about what she felt in her heart, regardless of how much I didn't want to tell her about what I found in the medical literature about her chance of survival.

Also in late May, I picked up the pace of visiting Margaret and noticed that she had taken a turn for the worse. According to the staff, she was eating less each day. I made it a point to bring along

Carrie's journal and read the entries in which Carrie wrote about how thankful she was for her parents.

I visited Margaret three times a day sometimes, and I read to her from the journal, from the letters, and from a college essay that Carrie wrote on motherhood, as well as the "Gone From My Sight" poem. I told Margaret that Carrie and Owen were on that distant shore looking for her, and that Carrie would be easy to see as she would be the one with the 10,000-watt smile. I do not know if Margaret understood what I was telling her, but I think she did. I do know it made me feel good just to sit with her and read those entries. I could hear Carrie's voice speaking through me along the way.

In early June, I decided to spend the night in the recliner next to Margaret's bed as she was in and out of consciousness. I was fortunate to be with her as she departed. If I were not present, I am not certain anyone would have noticed that she was gone. At the moment of her passing, all I could think of was that I wanted Margaret to let Carrie know how much I missed her, but somehow, I also knew that Carrie was watching over us at that moment.

Again, as with Carrie, I waited by Margaret's side to allow her spirit time to move along before I went down the hall to the nurse station to inform them of her passing.

At Margaret's celebration of life service in Ohio, I talked about finding Carrie's journal, about how Margaret was such an influence in launching Carrie out into the world as an independent, confident, and God-loving woman. The entire discussion took about fifteen minutes, much less time than my lengthy discussion at Carrie's service.

Margaret's service was a simple affair conducted at the cemetery, with a lunch afterwards at a nearby restaurant. Friends and family members told stories about Owen and Margaret, and of course, Carrie. As we wrapped up the lunch, the last to leave were

Don and Laurie, along with Laurie's mom, Ginger, who had been Margaret's friend for over seventy years. Ginger reminded me that I will never find anyone like Carrie. Not sure if that was an admonition to not even bother trying or just a statement of the obvious. Nevertheless, Ginger was spot on, and if I ever do meet someone else down the road that I want to share my quickly dwindling middle and old age with, it will be according to a different paradigm. Regardless, it will be a new frontier as expectations in my late sixties are appropriately different from those first twenty or so trips around the sun. I think that Carrie would want me to move forward and not fret about what she would think, as she knew I would not abandon the memories I have with her.

Shortly after returning from Margaret's service, I found another strange "gift" on what would have been Carrie's sixty-fifth birthday. It had been in our home since 2006: a history of the Ox College dormitory by Diane Stemper that was stashed under other items on a bookcase. I had never given it much attention until that day. The history included short contributions from former residents, and I was surprised to find an entry from Carrie describing her experience in 1976:

WRITTEN SOMETIME IN 2006

I spent my entire career as a resident of Oxford College. I can still remember unpacking in August of 1976. I was a naïve co-ed from McDonald High School. Due mostly to complicated roommate problems and a severe bout of homesickness, by September, I was positive that Miami was not the place for me. However, the nurturing environment of Ox College fostered a sense of belonging that caused my homesickness to be relieved. By January, I was applying to be a Resident Assistant.

My second year was spent on the second floor of Ox College with a roommate I still consider a friend. We were responsible for the adjustment of a new batch of coeds, and I think my rough start the previous year prepared me well for this challenge. I enjoyed the experience so much I applied to be the Student Assistant for the following year.

I sometimes wonder if I sheltered myself in some way by remaining only at Ox College for my entire three years at Miami, I doubt if this naïve freshman would have remained in Oxford if it were not for the comfort I felt each time I walked up the steps to the inviting white doors of my home away from home.

What a great find for me on Carrie's birthday. If Carrie had told me back in 2006 of her contribution to this small booklet, I had forgotten about it over the intervening seventeen years. Somehow, I think it was one of the many things she did quietly and without fanfare—a sort of gift to herself. Good for Carrie.

During the intervening months, I benefited from many kind gestures and interactions. Regular visits, notes, and dinner invitations from so many people helped prevent me from isolating myself. More importantly, the simple act of talking with others who knew and appreciated Carrie provided an outlet of unquantifiable value.

Frederick Health Hospice invited me to a surviving spouse support group. It was timed such that the group members were not new to their feelings, and that participants had ample awareness of what they experienced. While the materials presented in the group setting did not come under the category of rocket science, it was packaged in such a way as to present many of the feelings I had experienced in an organized manner. What I most benefited from was the interaction with others who had endured the same sort of loss. In eight short weeks, we bonded from a group of seven strangers to a group of people with a collective understanding of the shared experiences that brought us together, and we learned tremendously from each other. The group did take a few weeks to get on track—the normal group dynamics were at play. But after the facilitator took us through discussion points where we were encouraged but not required to contribute, we found commonality, but we also appreciated the unique aspects of each other's loss. I was the junior member of the group and initially felt a little out of place, but I soon appreciated the wisdom expressed by my fellow group members.

Regardless of the many social interactions, the physical workouts at CrossFit, my engagements with colleagues at work, proximity to my two great sons living nearby, and the discovery of a prayer room close to my home, there was still no way to escape the grief process. I hurt for several months, but it would have been substantially worse had I not taken advantage of all the lifelines. And spending time by myself in reflection and putting thoughts together for this book also helped. In that process, I am thankful for the assistance of a writing coach from an unlikely source: Oxford, Ohio. When I set up a scholarship in Carrie's memory, the point person from the development office inquired whether there was anything Miami University could do for me, and I asked if they had any resources that could help me with my writing. He put me in touch with Laura, who I worked with via Zoom calls. Laura evolved into part writing coach and part therapist. In some strange way, we quickly established a mutual understanding. Laura's office was in a converted off-campus dormitory—the building that Carrie lived in for her three years at Miami. Laura's daughter went to the same school where Carrie was a student teacher. And Laura's first book was based on a tragic loss she endured. Laura "got me." Upon reviewing my first draft, she pushed me to look inward and describe what I was thinking through the many life events. And through a period of several months and some tearful discussions with Laura, I was able to work through a good portion of my grieving by writing about it.

JANUARY 6, 1977

I constantly wonder if my existence will ever mean anything to anybody. I know we're not all destined to become world leaders and the like, but how can I measure my success in life? Who's to say that a simple, quiet life isn't successful? I want to be a teacher. If I'm a really good teacher, I will influence hundreds of children in my lifetime (if God grants me a full life). I'll have a hand in molding their characters. Isn't that a worthy lifestyle? I know it is—from now on, no more doubts. I'm going to be the best school teacher around. That's my goal, and with God's help and a little drive, I'll get there!

The Things Carrie Saved

Carrie maintained two big collections of letters and cards from students. The big collections represent bookends on her career in education and counseling. Thanks to Carrie's mentor at Kramer Elementary in Oxford, Ohio, in 1979, the entire fourth-grade class wrote letters to Carrie on the last day of school. An interesting finding in these letters was the neat cursive handwriting of the students, something that kids do not currently learn, as keyboarding is taught from an early age. Two themes jump out from the Kramer Elementary students. First, a common appreciation for a poetry project that Carrie had them work on during her time in that classroom, and second, the students' anticipation of Carrie's return to Kramer the next year, as it was common knowledge that Carrie had been offered a job in that building. One student went so far as to comment that Carrie was the prettiest teacher they ever had. Unfortunately for the kids at Kramer Elementary, Carrie would go on to take the junior high school teaching position in Columbiana the following year.

The other correspondence is a collection of retirement cards that were made by eighth graders that Carrie counseled at Crestwood Middle School. These young people, separated by forty years from Carrie's students at Kramer Elementary, appreciated that she had helped them to identify solutions to their own problems. They also wrote that she never belittled their problems, including those they had at home, and that she was calm, friendly, available, and approachable. Most importantly, there were many notes of genuine concern and best wishes for Carrie to beat her cancer. All these cards were in block letters—no cursive in 2015.

And what did Carrie save from me? Saved in her journal was the card I gave her when she started her first teaching job at Columbiana. I also found the card I gave her at graduation from Miami, where I acknowledged that I would support her with any future educational endeavor she decided to pursue. Last was a letter I wrote to her in 2010 as part of a church program for writing letters to your kids, with the first one to be directed to your spouse. In that 2010 letter, I acknowledged that the timing of the year spent in Korea was not perfect and that if I'd had that choice to do over again, things would be different. I also concluded by stating that each day Carrie was more beautiful and exciting to live with than the previous day. Maybe that's why she saved that letter.

Several friends and colleagues throughout Carrie's life sent me a few thoughts about Carrie. Consistent themes could be found across the spectrum of college friends, a friend from our Army days, and from Frederick friends. *Optimistic, Fun, Caring, Dedicated, Dependable, and Encouraging.* These characteristics were identified by several friends over the years. The college friends predicted she would be a great teacher, and her teaching friends described how she *was* one—and they frequently noted how effortlessly she maintained control of the classroom. One friend wrote that she waited a while to send me something because, in writing down her thoughts, she would need to admit to herself that Carrie was gone from this world.

So, there we have the answer to one of Carrie's early questions: Will my existence matter? Carrie's existence on this earth indeed mattered! Carrie did not need to be a world leader to make it so. Instead, Carrie mattered to many students, friends, and family—to each of us in her own special way. And to me, her life partner, she was my advisor, conscience, and encourager. I am not certain that my many professional opportunities would have been possible without Carrie speaking subliminally—sometimes whispering and sometimes doing more obvious things, like dropping the employment section from the *Washington Post* on my lap on that cozy Sunday morning in November 2006.

Carrie had many gifts, but there was one that qualified as a superpower: her smile. That smile could melt hearts, open doors, disarm adversaries, and control a classroom. Complimenting that smile were perfect teeth and wide eyes. She never had orthodontia as a child and rarely squinted when she smiled. I could never figure out the latter part, as whenever I smile, my eyes almost automatically narrow. And the brightness of the smile—to say it put out 10,000 watts is an understatement.

Carrie did not always flash that smile but rather employed it with great discretion. She used it in social situations when meeting people for the first time to demonstrate a friendly demeanor and communicate an openness that encouraged friendship. She used it in group settings when serving on volunteer boards to let others know that she was open to their ideas. She used it in the classroom to great effect to let students know that she thought they were important and that she wanted them to learn. In counseling sessions with middle schoolers, she smiled to help students open up to her about problems they were experiencing. With our boys, it was a way to communicate love from their mother. And to me, it meant many things. Most importantly, it meant she was happy to be with me.

Oh, how I miss that smile.

And it makes me appreciate that much more Carrie's decision to forge a life with me.

And as I now move forward, I think back on the many things I learned about and from Carrie, both when she was alive and through her death. A good discussion for a closing chapter.

JULY 19, 1978

I guess that's what making a commitment is all about.

CHAPTER 10

What Matters in the End

I want to live with myself and so
I want to be fit for myself to know
I want to be able as days go by
always to look myself in the eye
I know what others may never know
I never can fool myself and so,
whatever happens, I want to be
self-respecting and conscience-free

– Edgar A. Guest

Atul Gawande, in his book, *Being Mortal: Medicine and What Matters in the End*, tells two stories: one from the public health perspective of a population faced with difficult situations as they age and cope with death, and one from his personal experience with his father throughout his final challenging years. We gave Ben a copy of the book for Christmas in 2014 when he was in medical school, but I read it first before wrapping it up. In 2014, we were still early into Carrie's initial relapse, and I did not fully appreciate all of the points made by Dr. Gawande. But I would come back to that book time and again in the last two years of Carrie's life. I would recommend Dr. Gawande's book to anyone looking to better understand end-of-life medical and emotional considerations.

Carrie lived well with cancer for over thirteen of the fifteen years of her disease. But those last two years, especially the last nine months, were plagued with treatment-related problems. In December 2020, when Carrie embarked on her battle with the third occurrence, her physical and mental status were strong and well-adjusted. Within four months, she would be in a coma and besieged with multiple side effects. After recovering from that misadventure, Carrie would continue on a gradual downhill slide until her fall in June 2022, resulting in a debilitating case of colitis. She was no longer sliding toward the edge. Her condition was akin to falling off a cliff. Carrie's radiation-injured left leg and broken left shoulder prevented her from getting out of bed, while anything that went into her body quickly passed through, thereby necessitating frequent bedding changes. Carrie absolutely hated the fact that she was the patient who needed to hit the nurse call button for the degrading exercise of cleanup of human excrement. It is no wonder why Carrie, when presented with the option to pursue a fourth different treatment to stop the colitis, after learning it would take a few weeks to work, opted for an ileostomy. And when the ostomy became a source of a potentially life-threatening infection, Carrie was terrified of the thought of going back to the hospital for the surgery to reverse the procedure.

What happened between December 2020 and June 2022 that would cause such a precipitous decline? A question with no answer. My assessment of the situation was that, given the nearly six years of positive response to the immunotherapy treatment while enrolled in the NCI protocol, it was assumed that the new combination would bypass the issue of resistance and that the risks of the new therapy would be similar to what Carrie had experienced at the NIH. However, the new treatment combination would conspire against Carrie in ways that could not have been predicted.

Did either Carrie or I have the appropriate appreciation for what it would be like to experience the known risks that were not seen in her NIH treatments? Not really. In the list of known possible side effects from the class of monoclonal antibodies and kinase inhibitors administered during Carrie's NCI treatment, she had few episodic problems. But these events were transient and controlled with symptomatic treatments. Given Carrie's history with immunotherapy at the NCI, I discounted the potential of bad things happening with the regimen proposed in 2021. However, clinical trials of the new therapy did not involve patients who had previously failed a combination similar to Carrie's. We were venturing into uncharted waters.

As someone not directly involved in patient care, I never previously witnessed the ramifications of any of the various treatments in an around-the-clock setting. Regardless of the degrading visual image of colitis in a patient confined to bed, perhaps someone should have recorded on video Carrie at her worst so that future patients can better appreciate the devastating possible effects of colitis. And I say this not as a downer, but to put into perspective that it is challenging to adequately describe these low-probability events.

In retrospect, if I had asked Carrie in February or March 2023 if she would have gone down the same path if she had better understood what she would encounter, what kind of answer would I have received? Would Carrie have weighed the opportunity to hold her granddaughter in her arms as something that would compensate for the suffering she endured?

And with this question, I look at lessons learned in graduate school. One of the disciplines of my graduate school training was in the realm of outcomes research and the utilization of patient preferences in medicine. In the last few decades, with newer treatments for cancer, the application of outcomes research in determining the role of a new treatment in the practice of medicine is becoming more routine.

Not surprisingly, patients and the public prefer medicines that do not cause hair loss, profound nausea and vomiting, and immediate threats to life from red and white blood cell disruptions that are frequently side effects of the traditional chemotherapy agents. This does not mean that the newer agents are risk-free. There are substantial risks, but they occur in ways that are different from first-line chemotherapy. And given that the clinical trials conducted to obtain approval for the newer agents could not account for every possible prior drug given to a patient, it is challenging to forecast the cumulative impact of the interactions that could occur with multiple medicines prescribed over time. And this is especially true when it comes to multiple immunotherapy agents, as their effects can linger on for an indeterminate time.

This situation of wandering into uncharted territory for medical care is often referred to as the data-free zone. This is why it was made clear to Carrie when she started her final treatment that it was a form of palliative care—an effort to reduce the burden of cancer, but it was not really known whether it would lead to a cure. What remained for Carrie was an uncertain hope that this new treatment would help reduce the burden of her disease.

And Carrie was fortunate up to this point. She had lived abundantly with cancer prior to this last relapse. Much credit goes to Carrie's lifelong interest in maintaining a certain degree of physical stamina and a strong social network. Recall how I wrote about Carrie having a long walk to school? While it wasn't like the tall tale of the Depression era kids walking four miles uphill to school both ways, Carrie's trek accounted for three miles of walking per day at a swift pace. Walking was a good habit to get into, and one that Carrie continued until late 2020 with the initiation of the third treatment regimen.

Additionally, Carrie had a well-developed social network. In addition to our family, near and far, Carrie was well connected with friends from our neighborhood, her book clubs, our church, two cancer support groups, and the two schools where she worked while in Frederick. There were also friends from McDonald and from our various Army assignments who checked up on her through phone and email. All these social interactions played an important part in maintaining Carrie's outlook on life.

Many of the individuals in her larger support sphere prayed for Carrie, which, regardless of your belief system, produced a positive effect as Carrie knew that others cared enough to pray for intervention from a higher power.

Physical strength and social interactions are important components of a lifestyle that typically helps us to experience our best possible life until we reach our final days. In his book, *Outlive*, Peter Attia introduces the concept of health span as a way of envisioning the healthy years in a lifespan. Dr. Attia's recommendation for having our health span mirror our lifespan does not come under the category of a medical mystery. Rather, it represents the things we need to do in our lives to ward off disease. In the case of someone like Carrie, it made it possible to live productively after the burden of disease onset. In his book, Dr. Attia backs up his concepts with data from multiple sources, so it warrants consideration among skeptics. *Outlive* was published long after Carrie was initially diagnosed, but Carrie intuitively knew that her best chance for maintaining her well-being was to do things that contributed to general good functioning as long as possible—those long walks, the social interactions, plenty of sleep, and proper diet. It wasn't until those last two years that the health span and lifespan curves separated.

In the final analysis, the bargain Carrie made to take her chances with the various treatments did provide her with over twelve years of productive life and nearly fifteen complete years that she would not have otherwise experienced. At the end of her life, having witnessed the arrival of her first grandchild, I think Carrie would agree that it was worth the effort to charge forward with eyes wide open into that third treatment regimen. Future patients will have their own situations to evaluate, but can learn from people like Carrie, who had many years living abundantly with cancer before weathering severe storms. Regardless, as Carrie knew, she was at peace with her Maker. What did matter to her in the end was the opportunity to take part in one of life's great joys—being a grandmother. Carrie knew in her heart what mattered in the end!

Moving Forward

Be yourself but be your best self
Dare to be different and follow your own star
And don't be afraid to be happy
Enjoy what is beautiful
Love with all your heart and soul
Believe that those you love, love you
Learn to forgive yourself for your faults
For this is the first step in learning to forgive others

– Attributed to Max Ehrmann

FEBRUARY 3, 1977

I've just got to make the best of every day, and life will be worthwhile even though it's flying!

The Path to Moving Forward

A big mistake that many people make when attempting to console a friend who has lost a loved one is to use the phrase, "You will eventually move on from so and so . . . "

Regardless of the well-meaning nature of the message, those words are unbelievably off target. We never really move on from the loss of our loved one. We learn to move forward. And moving forward is a path that is far from straight. It is filled with detours, traffic jams, and confusing signs. And the trail is different for everyone.

My journey, which will go on for the remainder of my life, was initially filled with long reflections on the life I had with Carrie. And the first connection to that life was the relationship I had with her parents, Owen and Margaret.

Growing up in a large family of ten kids provided me with a concrete set of values, as well as a certain amount of resilience and flexibility. But the interactions with Owen and Margaret would teach me the routines of living a normal life—having dinner at a certain time every day, keeping things organized and tidy, following a family budget, and looking out for the greater community through volunteer activities. Of course, it helped tremendously that Owen and Margaret were focused on Carrie and wanted her to grow up and have a great life. And somehow, they recognized in me that I would be a good match for their daughter. They did many things to encourage our relationship, but at the same time, they wanted Carrie to grow independently. For example, they intuitively knew that nothing good would come of Carrie going to Ohio State, where I was enrolled. They wanted Carrie to succeed on her own and not end up getting married or pregnant—or both—before she graduated. Yet, when Carrie was in McDonald, they wanted me to be present for most family events. They probably helped Carrie form the mindset she expressed in her journal on Valentine's Day 1977: "Will what we have last forever?" The answer at that time was to "wait and see." When we eventually determined that we would become committed to each other, Owen and Margaret did everything possible to encourage us along that path.

And then there was my relationship with Margaret, which was qualitatively different than my relationship with the couple, Owen and Margaret. Early in the time that we were engaged, Margaret asked to see me for a few minutes—alone. She had one simple question. What was I going to call her? I had not given the matter much thought. Up until that time, Owen was always Owen, as everyone in town called him by that name. However, I referred to Margaret as Mrs. Ague. I knew that Margaret referred to her mother-in-law as "mom," so I told her that I would call her "mom," but not until after Carrie and I were married. Margaret was thrilled to hear that answer. And from that day on, Margaret started treating me like a son. Margaret and I had a very special relationship, and some of that may have been knowing that Carrie could at times be a difficult person to live with. Margaret appreciated that I rarely let Carrie's mood swings alter my lasting love.

Losing Carrie and Margaret within ten weeks of each other tossed my otherwise even-keeled perspective on life off-kilter. And upon reflection, I realized that the combination of the two losses chipped away at a mental foundation that was built over a lifetime.

I would like to think that I had a reservoir of resilience that prevented depression, but as with any resource, that lake got fairly close to empty. As I conclude this book and look at my future, I recognize and appreciate that there is only so much I can do by myself, and even with the help already received, I need to continue to take action to repair the cracks and allow the reservoir to refill.

Reflections on Carrie

Carrie, though she was a perfectionist, had her imperfections, just as I have mine. We accepted each other's faults and lived with them. Sometimes we complained about the minor and major irritations, but most of the time we just remained silent—and we continued to love each other because that is what you do in a committed relationship. And when life was not perfect, causing anxiety in Carrie, the imperfections were not deal breakers. I wonder how Carrie would have described my imperfections.

Neither of us was ever unfaithful to the other, but at this time, I have started to notice females again. And an explanation of that last sentence: During Carrie's last nine months, I was the primary caregiver. While the aides gave her bed baths, I was involved in the ostomy care and other activities that forced me to put on hold any emotions I had regarding Carrie's body—a form that remained special to me throughout her lifetime. My detachment was a defense mechanism and was effective in keeping me focused on my caregiving duties. That shield is no longer required, and I can again appreciate the female form.

About our forty-three-year marriage: We didn't shout and scream at each other. We didn't spend money behind each other's backs. We didn't use drugs or abuse alcohol. We sometimes had disagreements regarding child rearing or the amount of time

I spent at work. A couple of times Carrie really blew up—once due to the stress of a move, and another time due to the inconsiderate behavior of the boys and me. It was like watching a kettle boil over without the whistling. It was an imperfection on her part. However, imperfect people who can accept the faults in those they love can make things work for a lifetime.

In an entry from early January 1977, Carrie noted that in her life she could have the opportunity to influence hundreds of children, with the following caveat: " . . . if God grants me a full life." Carrie did positively influence children: as a teacher, as a counselor, and as the mother of boys—and to the friends of those boys. As to the question of a full life, the answer is mixed. Until Carrie's third ordeal with cancer, she lived a full life almost every day. Note that I said "almost every day." There were times in her life when she was either depressed or anxiety-ridden, but those were relatively short and self-corrected.

Was her life long? That is a different matter. I recall as a young person reading the obituary section of the newspaper, thinking that it was not uncommon for people to pass away in their mid-sixties, and thinking of those people as old. However, my frame of reference on this topic has shifted substantially as I am now in the latter part of my sixth decade. The amateur demographer in me thinks middle age begins at sixty-five and old age at eighty-five. As such, Carrie was denied some of the things that we all look forward to in those healthy years before old age slows us down: watching grandchildren grow up, traveling at a leisurely pace, being with friends and family through good times and bad, and the continued companionship with a life partner.

In two of the journal entries, Carrie notes that she would like to be half as good at raising children as her parents were at raising her. Now, as a grandfather, I realize that comparisons of parenthood across generations are impossible. Carrie's childhood in sleepy McDonald, Ohio, was relatively isolated, and it was easy to protect her from some of the bad influences that could corrupt her. Nevertheless, the challenges that we faced as parents, moving our boys around the world, would not be a fair comparison. And our kids were fortunate enough to go through high school before the big booms in social media. Similarly, it would be impossible for Ben to compare my parenthood to his as he raises Fern. We have no idea what challenges the world will present to Ben, Renee, and Fern. This would have been a good topic for discussion with a healthy Carrie had I known about the presence of her journal, especially given Carrie's experience as a school counselor. Nonetheless, Carrie was a good parent, albeit not a perfect parent, and, as she noted, neither were Owen and Margaret. Neither was I.

Regarding Carrie's question in her journal entry, written after we were engaged, about independence and travel, I know that Carrie experienced both. First, a note about Carrie's 1978 journal entry about independence. Carrie's frame of reference was that of Owen and Margaret's. And while Margaret was a strong person, Owen was, at times, like Archie Bunker regarding his expectations. Despite loving her parents and appreciating most everything about their union, Carrie knew that she would not enter a lifelong relationship as a doting wife. Carrie wanted more out of marriage and life. We were partners in our marriage. Our regular routines at home were, for the most part, in a state of synchronized sinus rhythms. From the time that Carrie wrote the conclusion to her meandering thoughts in July 1978 and stated, "I guess that is what commitment is all about," she was fully on board and stayed that way, and so did I.

Carrie grew more beautiful every day, in the classic sense that beauty means more than outward appearance. In my eyes, though, she also grew more physically attractive. Carrie's confidence and friendly demeanor allowed her to radiate a beauty that is difficult to describe. With her long, slender neck and willowy stature, it is not too much of a stretch to say that she grew from the ungainly cygnet in her sophomore year of high school into the picture of the radiant swan. It also didn't hurt that her smile was dazzling. Even as Carrie entered those last difficult years of her life, she was able to maintain that smile.

And as a last reflection, it becomes more evident to me every day that we lived many lives and versions of ourselves in our forty-nine-year relationship, beginning with that time when Carrie sat behind me in trigonometry. While we didn't know if we were in love during those first six years before marriage, we did so afterwards. And with each version of ourselves, we learned to accept the change, but the one thing that remained constant was an increasing love for one another.

What we did appreciate was the understanding that we could not take our marriage for granted. We worked hard to maintain our relationship every day (or at least nearly every day). We made each other the number one human priority in the other's life, and that helped make the changes in our respective lives seem imperceptible. It would probably not be possible for me to have realized some of these things when Carrie was still alive, but during this new post-Carrie existence, I have the benefit of putting together the many pieces and figuring out the many versions of life we shared, and each was memorable.

Regrets

Part of the process of moving forward is to learn to let go of my regrets. And to do that, I first needed to enumerate the real and perceived faults that I hold fast in my conscience.

First, I often chastise myself for not doing more to prevent the fall that Carrie experienced in June 2022. Could I have made the bathroom a safer place for Carrie? Or should I have perhaps moved us out of that house and into a one-level home free of any stairs? The one thing that helps me move beyond this regret is the presence of the note on the poem Carrie left in her nightstand regarding the imagery of death. Even if I could have somehow prevented the fall on that June morning, Carrie was already on a terminal decline, and the question to be resolved comes down to the steepness of that descent. As such, when this issue comes up in my pea-sized brain as I am trying to fall asleep, I have managed to come to peace with the inevitability of the final outcome.

A second regret is somewhat more difficult to shake off. As the day approached for Carrie's ostomy reversal surgery in January 2023, she expressed anxiety over whether the procedure would work. And as described previously, I reassured her there was nothing to worry about. I could not have been more wrong. This regret is something that will take substantially more time to come to terms with, as Carrie's fears were far more legitimate than I ever fathomed.

A third weight I carry with me is our failure to talk about death—not so much that the discussion would be about death but rather an appreciation for the life we had together. Had we accepted the inevitable before Carrie entered hospice, perhaps we could have pulled out her wonderful picture albums and scrapbooks and taken a well-deserved trip down memory lane together. At this point, I kick myself for not making it a priority to go through those books with Carrie so I could tell her just how much I appreciated that she decided to share her life with me, resulting in the many great memories we shared.

Fourth, I was too caught up in attempting to be the reliable caregiver who met Carrie's physical needs with her limited mobility, ostomy support, and medication management. However, my focus on the physical resulted in an imaginary curtain that separated me from Carrie's emotional needs. Perhaps this was a defense mechanism on my part, but I do ponder how I could have been more present to Carrie, especially during those times when she experienced increased anxiety. Other than holding her hand and sitting at her side, which I did on a regular basis, I wish there was more that I could have done in the domain of emotional support.

Fifth, I am not sure that I will ever be able to get over my lack of emotional strength when I yelled at Carrie during those early morning hours of March 12th, when she was thrashing about with a combination of anxiety and physical discomfort. My perceived need for sleep should have taken a back seat to the immediate needs of Carrie. In retrospect, it is possible that my reaction was due to a whiplash effect of moving from the person who was helping keep Carrie alive to the person aiding in her ultimate death. The emotional toll of the different extremes of caregiving has both short-term and long-term effects. The short-term emotional response was immediately evident, but I am only now beginning to grapple with the longer-term aspects. Coming to grips with this will take considerable time and may become another story unto itself. Nevertheless, it is not a worthy excuse for the short-term response of overreacting in those early morning hours of March 12th.

Did I say any of this to Carrie while she was alive? Maybe. In small bits and awkward pieces, for as a male, my capacity to express my innermost thoughts is often inhibited by the fact that my chromosomes do not match.

Last, a common reaction that many have expressed after providing long-term care for a loved one is a sense of relief that the long vigil is over. I noted at the outset of this book that no one could want to see suffering continue. However, if the human suffering could have been better managed, I would have wanted very much for Carrie to remain with me to experience events such as Fern's first birthday. This last regret is similar to the whiplash described in the previous paragraph. At times, I feel selfish that I experienced relief from the demands of my physical involvement in keeping Carrie alive. What a conundrum of human emotions.

Learning to Forgive Myself

There are some items that I have already rationalized for which I can forgive myself, and others where it may be more challenging to ever get to that point. What I do know is that Carrie, in the entries she made in the poetry section of her journal in 1977, provided advice in this area. In particular were the last lines paraphrased from a poem she attributed to Max Ehrmann:

Learn to forgive yourself for your faults
For this is the first step in learning to forgive others

A second source to inspire self-forgiveness came from **Lectio 365**, a daily devotional app by Pete Greig and associates. In one of the daily devotions, Pete provided the simple admonition to choose not to wallow in failure or regret. That sage advice stays with me. Regardless of the advice, I still felt a need to capture my guilt in writing. A few months after Carrie passed, I reduced that tally of regrets to a list of bullets that I wrote down and put into my wallet—sort of like carrying around a weight (a common Biblical theme and used in song by the late Robbie Robertson). I knew that at some point, I would be ready to give up that "load," and it happened in a somewhat accidental manner. But does anything really happen by accident?

In the spring of 2024, a widow friend with far longer experience told me that she was at the local prayer room where they were burning old prayers. She asked if I was ready to let go of my perceived faults. If I was ready, wouldn't sending them up in flames, similar to the collection of the prayers of others, be an appropriate way? As the passage of time had lessened the weight of my burden, I realized I was ready. The communal environment of reading my list around others prior to burning allowed me to surrender my burden.

Maintaining Faith

I concluded my remarks at Carrie's celebration of life service by noting that while Carrie had undergone several assaults on her well-being, she retained her faith in God. And I went on to explain that Carrie was not one to boast about her faith, but to try to live her faith through a quiet example. I would say that, for the most part, I have tried to do the same. However, I would be dishonest if I did not admit the events of the last few years have caused challenges to that foundation of faith. Watching Carrie go through her cancer and the treatment-related problems was not an easy process. Questioning how it is that Carrie had to go through the slow and painful ordeal is a natural reaction. Additionally, being deprived of the opportunity to see her granddaughter grow up tore at Carrie's heart. And from my selfish perspective, I lost the opportunity of continued life with my much-loved partner. We had so many things left to see and do together, especially as I feel that we were just hitting middle age.

Again, I return to Carrie's journal for some guidance and solace in facing middle and old age without her by my side. Carrie, as a young person, astutely observed in nine different entries the phenomenon of time flying by. From both a metaphysical and spiritual perspective, though, we know that our existence is relatively short in the grand order of things. Moreover, in the book *Reality*

Is Not What It Seems, the Italian physicist Carlo Rovelli includes a chapter on the topic that time does not exist. Even though time on Earth can be discretely quantified, astrophysicists are flummoxed when attempting to quantify the age of the universe, thus making discernment of time in metaphysical terms somewhat challenging. This paradox regarding the construct of time on Earth and across the universe supports, in a roundabout way, the Judeo-Christian belief that God is the beginning and the end—an agreement between science and religion, sort of. As such, it also reinforces our understanding that there is a force much greater than a random big bang that brought us to our place on Earth. And that keeps the door open for my beliefs.

For that reason, I follow the Hebrews 11:1 definition that faith is the hope of things that cannot be seen and of things to come. And while that verse is about the hope we place in salvation, one of those other things to come is the hope that I will encounter Carrie's spirit after I depart this world—even though there will not be a day in which I will not miss Carrie while still a part of this life.

NOVEMBER 17, 1977

I've learned a lot about myself—my shortcomings and my ability to deal with problems I never thought I could handle.

Moving Forward

So, how do I move forward from here? As of this writing, over two years after Carrie passed, I have found contentment with life. Yes, I do still struggle at times, but for the most part, I am at peace. Am I happy, or do I experience joy? Those are different concepts.

Happiness is something we encounter with a given experience. So, yes, I can report that I am happy to be with my kids, my granddaughter Fern, and friends. Joy, on the other hand, is on a different scale from the happiness domain. Joy is much like contentment. It involves a choice. You either are content or you are not. You are either at the level of consciousness of joy or not. Achieving joy is a steep cliff to climb. But with help, I am learning to find the important hand and toe holds necessary to achieve joy. Regardless, contentment is a good state in which to exist.

And as I am content, I want to keep Carrie's memory alive as I move forward. Writing this book was part of that process, but there are other ways I hope will help in that process. One thing I look forward to in the coming years will be reading to Fern those letters from Carrie's friends about their memories of Carrie.

During the last several months, I met with many widows, widowers, and friends who've lost a child. Their respective journeys helped provide perspective. I consumed many cups of coffee while listening appreciatively to the various insights expressed by these fellow travelers. I am also appreciative that my sons and siblings have been very supportive, and that I retain the extended Ague clan as part of my family. While the Frederick Health Hospice spousal support group was a good experience for me, I now find that participating as a hospice volunteer and providing an ear for people who are at the end of their life journey is a most rewarding experience.

Finally, I recognized that I need to remain in a state of gratitude for the life I had with Carrie. Does this mean I no longer grieve for my loss? Absolutely not. I grieve every day, but I don't let it consume me. Instead, having gratitude as the foundation keeps Carrie's memory alive as a positive beacon. At times, I hear Carrie's voice in my head whispering encouragement in this regard. Carrie wants me to move forward. And live a full life.

CARRIE'S JOURNAL – JANUARY 4, 1977

Sure, I know that on this date such and such happened to me, but I don't know how I felt when I was honored or perhaps defeated—from now on, I will.

Acknowledgements

This book would not have been possible had it not been for the discovery made by Sissy Plank and Karen Pierson while helping me clear out Carrie's things after her death. Those two people helped tremendously throughout Carrie's life, but especially during her illness and in my transition after her death. They continue to be a source of encouragement.

Carrie's friends from Miami University helped pull cobwebs out of my brain. Props go to Mary Lynne Pallasch, Dewey Yoder Ford, Nancy Andres, and Brenda Scholl for helping to fill in the blanks from the 1970s when Carrie wrote the bulk of her entries.

I gained tremendous insight into loss from widows and widowers through sitting for a cup of coffee, real or virtual, as some of these individuals live in distant locations. Widow friends, including Peg Bruckart, Laura Brosch, Claire McMahon Morgan, my cousin Mary Cay Somerville, Carolyn True, and Carrie's college friend, Mary Lynne Pallasch, also fall into this category. My widower friends, Pete Marinello, Don Van Duyn, and Patrick Castranova, were similarly helpful.

Parents who lost a child are a special group unto themselves, as I cannot begin to understand that level of loss. Regardless, Jane Talarico, Michael Paskowsky, Greg Berezuk, Bob Viti, and my brother Joe were able to share with me on their respective journeys. Perspectives gained from these diverse experiences helped me identify ways to navigate my journey.

Amy and Deb Jefferson invited me to their home on the Pungo River in North Carolina during the time I prepared my initial draft. That much-needed break helped recharge my brain before heading back to my writing task.

Susan Kloc, a neighbor in Clover Hill, put together a collection of "letters for Fern" from Carrie's friends. This collection helped me to recall many of Carrie's tremendous qualities and helped me double-check timeline events. I look forward to reading those letters to Fern so that she will know how special Grandma Carrie was to so many people.

Matthew Jones, a development officer at Miami University, followed through on the strange request I had about the availability of assistance from a faculty member who could help me with my writing. Matthew introduced me to Laura Gaddis, a visiting professor at Miami, who also conducts workshops for aspiring writers at the Oxford Community Arts Center and coaches writers online through lauragaddis.com. Though my meetings with Laura were through Zoom, she intuited my needs and would transition from writing coach to therapist as the situation required. Laura helped me take my initial 110,000-word catharsis and encouraged me to expound on my feelings and create scenes while taking a machete to content that did not contribute to the story. Somehow, through an addition by subtraction process, we whittled the words down to a manageable number with an appropriate organization.

I had several readers of early drafts who provided feedback: Linda Warehime, Fran Haller, Sheila McCullough, Linda Cofrancesco, Joan Miles (my high school typing teacher), Carol Ann Hart, and lastly, Bonnie Molnar. Bonnie was introduced to me by Joan and Carol Ann as a proof-reading maven—and she was. Bonnie helped me get my draft ready to send out to publishers. Bonnie, a big thanks!

I was fortunate to partner with Indigo River Publishing. Their professional approach cannot be overstated. Thanks to the team of Freya Murphy, River Chau, Keira Lopez, Deborah Froese, Anne MacDonald, and Dianna Graveman, who were all professional and positive. I especially appreciated Anne's ability to look at the content and reorganize it into what I hope is a compelling narrative. Dianna was superb in making the message come across in a clear, consistent voice. And Deborah masterfully orchestrated all parts of the editing process.

Many friends, here in Frederick, as well as Ohio and across the country, including relatives in the UK, provide encouragement in ways seen and unseen. The same can be said for the Brook Hill and Calvary United Methodist Church congregations. The Ague, Higham, Charles, and Pierson family lines are always a source of support. My sons, Dan and Ben, daughter-in-law Renee, and granddaughter Fern continue to provide motivation.

Last, thanks to Carrie for keeping that old leather-bound journal. You will never be forgotten. Thanks for inspiring me to move forward.

Pictures

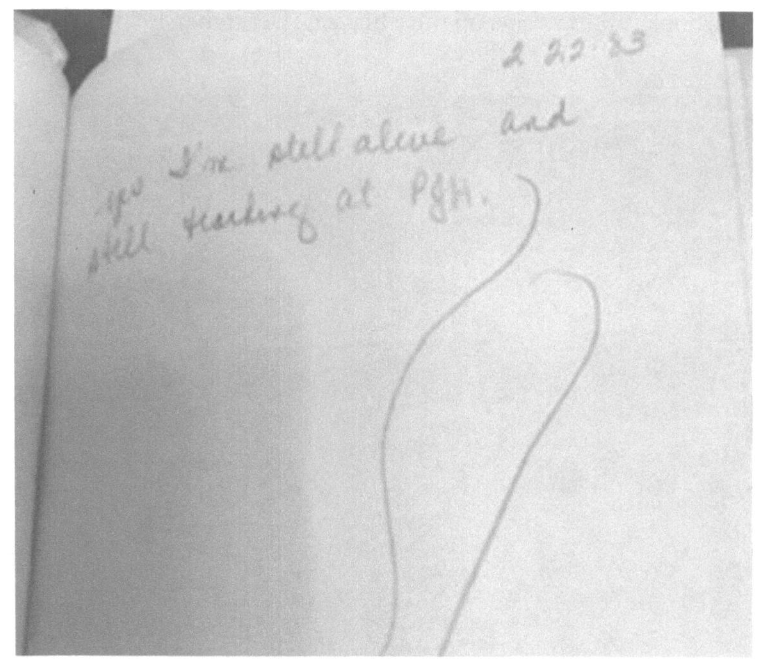

Yearbook caption sums up the situation (December 1974).

After Jerry's high school graduation (June 1975).

Carrie's nineteen birthday dinner with Pamela Sue, Cathy Jean, and Laurie Ella.

Carrie with coy smirk before the ROTC ball (February 1979).

My hair grown out after ROTC classes concluded (August 1979).

Dancing at our wedding (July 1980).

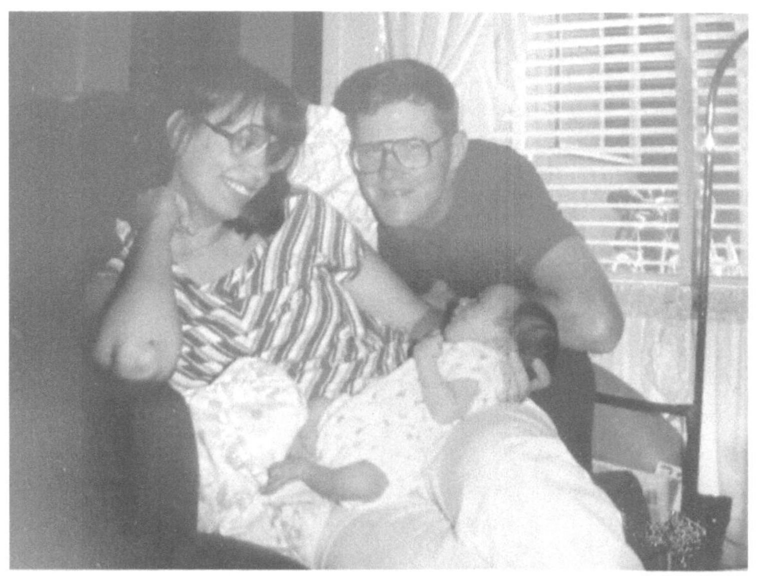

Doting on baby Danny (July 1985).

With the boys on top of the Zugspitze, Germany's highest point (October 1990).

On a hiking trail outside Zermatt, Switzerland, looking toward the Matterhorn (October 1992).

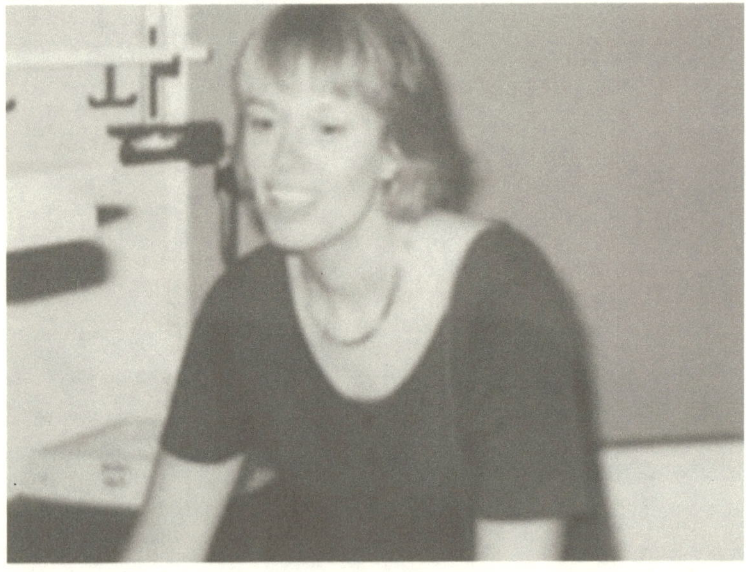

Back when the overhead projector was the way teachers delivered their lessons (1996).

Carrie at her master's degree graduation from Western Maryland with guest speaker, the late Cokie Roberts. Carrie and Cokie would later run into each other on a regular basis in the waiting room of the NCI clinic (May 2002).

Dan and Ben at the Korean DMZ (July 2002).

Carrie appreciating the boys on Mother's Day (May 2003).

Sissy, Margaret, and Carrie in Hawaii (September 2006).

Army Formal Function (August 2006).

Carrie's hair grew back thick after the first chemotherapy (October 2012).

Ben's graduation from AT Still Osteopathic in Mesa, Arizona, with Aunt Diane, Margaret, and Renee (May 2016).

Ben and Renee's wedding (April 2018).

Athabasca Glacier, Alberta, Canada (June 2019).

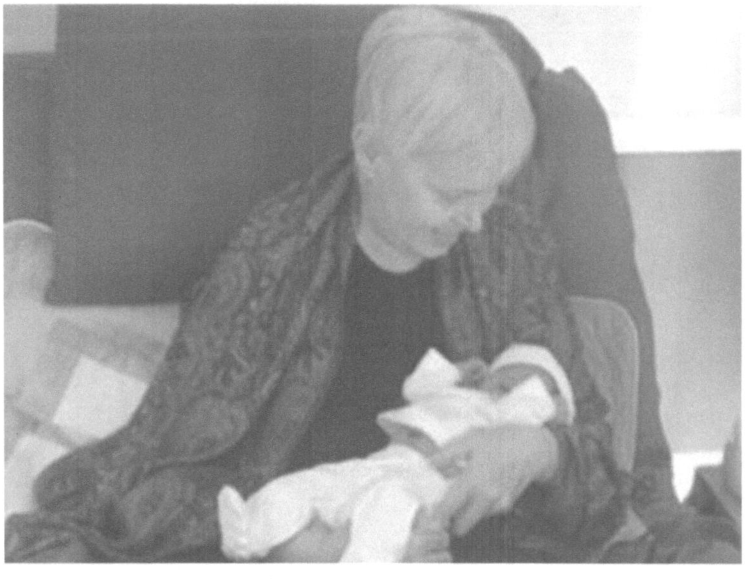

Carrie meets baby Fern (September 2022).

Carrie's smile (1980 and 2015).

References

Books

Attia, Peter, and Bill Gifford. *Outlive: The Science & Art of Longevity*. New York: Harmony, 2023.

Mukherjee, Siddhartha. *The Emperor of All Maladies*. London, England: Fourth Estate, 2011.

American Psychiatric Association. *Diagnostic and Statistical Manual of Mental Disorders*. 5th ed. Arlington, VA: American Psychiatric Association, 2013.

Gawande, Atul. *Being Mortal: Medicine and What Matters in the End*. New York: Metropolitan Books/Henry Holt and Company, 2014.

van der Kolk, Bessel A. *The Body Keeps the Score: Brain, Mind, and Body in the Healing of Trauma*. New York: Viking, 2014.

Rovelli, Carlo, Simon Carnell, and Erica Segre. *Reality Is Not What It Seems: The Journey to Quantum Gravity*. First American edition. New York: Riverhead Books, an imprint of Penguin Random House LLC, 2017.

Pamphlet

Stamper, Diane. *Building Memory, Inventing the Future – Year Book – A Collection of Images and Stories Charting the Historical Progress of a Building – College Ave & High St –Oxford, Ohio*. Oxford, OH: Ohio Arts Council, Oxford Community Foundation, and Oxford Community Arts Center, 2006.

Journal Articles

Osei-Tutu, A., A. Nunes, J. Lee, M. Yu, L. Hernandez, H. Chen, N. Takebe, N. Houston, I. Ekwede, S. Steinberg, J. Chen, L. Cao, W. Figg, D. Butcher, C. Annunziata, and E. Kohn. "A Phase I Dose Expansion Cohort Study of Dasatinib in Combination with Bevacizumab in Advanced Solid Tumors (NCT01445509)." *Journal of Clinical Oncology* 35 (2017): 2585. https://doi.org/10.1200/JCO.2017.35.15_suppl.2585.

Makker, Vicky, David Rasco, Nicholas Vogelzang, Marcia Brose, Alexander Cohn, Jason Mier, Christopher Simone, David Hyman, Deborah Stepan, Cristiana Dutcus, Erik Schmidt, Meng Guo, Prakash Sachdev, Robert Shumaker, Carol Aghajanian, and Matthew Taylor. "Lenvatinib plus Pembrolizumab in Patients with Advanced Endometrial Cancer: An Interim Analysis of a Multicentre, Open-Label, Single-Arm, Phase 2 Trial." *The Lancet Oncology* 20 (2019). https://doi.org/10.1016/S1470-2045(19)30020-8.

Film

Pollack, Sydney, and Phillipa Brathwaite, producers. *Sliding Doors.* Directed by Peter Howitt. Los Angeles: Intermedia / Mirage Enterprises, 1998.

Television

Lear, Norman, developer. *All in the Family.* 1971–1979. CBS Television.

Brooks, James L., and Allan Burns, developers. *The Mary Tyler Moore Show.* 1970–1977. MTM Enterprises and CBS Television.

Music

Larson, Jonathan. "Seasons of Love." From *Rent*, Broadway musical. 1996.

Robertson, Robbie. "The Weight." Performed by The Band. Released August 8, 1968. A&R Recorders, New York.

www.ingramcontent.com/pod-product-compliance
Lightning Source LLC
LaVergne TN
LVHW091052080826
845145LV00002B/712

* 9 7 8 1 9 6 9 9 3 5 0 9 1 *